*featuring the*
## "JUST HOUSE MANNERS" *Program*

# Good Dog!

## Simple Training for Successful Behavior

## DONNA CHANDLER

### CANINE TRAINER AND BEHAVIOR MODIFICATION SPECIALIST

emmis

**books**

Copyright © 2003 by Donna Chandler

All rights reserved. No portion of this book may be reproduced in any fashion, print, facsimile, or electronic, or by any method yet to be developed, without express permission of the copyright holder. For further information, contact the publisher at

Emmis Books
1700 Madison Road, 2nd Floor
Cincinnati, Ohio 45206

ISBN 1-57860-153-3

LCCN 2003112874


Interior and text design by Sheila G. Samson, WordCrafter, Inc., Carmel, Indiana

Interior photographs by Scott Mumphrey Photography, Indianapolis, Indiana: pages 7 (bottom), 16, 26, 30, 45, 58, 71, 76, 90 (top), and 100.

If you have questions or comments, feel free to contact me at

dgchickoryhall@earthlink.net

🐾 *Donna*

*To my husband, Greg, and my children — Jonas, Lolly, and Austin — for tolerating and supporting my love of animals.*

*Also, to all the puppies that have come into my life, especially Mac, Mandy, Thatcher, Savannah, Little Bear, and Ellie Mae.*

# Contents

# Foreword

You are about to embark on a most rewarding and entertaining adventure. I say adventure, because as you implement the exercises in *Good Dog!*, you and your family will cement the bond that will last through the life of your pet. Housebreaking and puppy education are just the beginning. You will have years of companionship to cherish. Donna Chandler provides the guidelines for establishing a healthy, respectful relationship with your pet, and she walks you through the basics which will give you the foundation for advanced training if you chose to pursue it. You cannot, however, have a champion obedience, tracking, or agility dog without the fundamentals that Donna outlines for you here.

As a veterinarian I counsel new pet owners on nutrition, preventative care and exercise. Aside from the health-related issues, the best advice I have given my clients is to read through *Good Dog!* and to begin immediately to incorporate training into their daily routines. I have two dogs of my own; the lessons provided here have been invaluable for their safety, the well being of my house, and the comfort of my guests. My dogs are not the most well-mannered dogs, but they do behave respectfully because of Donna's training methods. This book will be the reference you can return to time and again for refreshers. Your pets will actually look forward to the interaction with you and your family, and family members will want to spend more time with a pet that is well behaved and eager to learn.

The first step to having a lasting relationship with your pet is to know what is expected of you. So . . . come, sit, read! The adventure awaits you with your dog nearby.

Jeanette L. Floss, D.V.M., M.S.
Diplomat, the American College
of Theriogenologists

# Preface

I never dreamed that I would write a second book. Writing the first one (entitled *Just House Manners*) was like climbing a mountain. However, in the spring of 2001 I attended and graduated from a course, "Dogs, Principles, and Techniques of Behavior Modification," at Purdue University in Lafayette, Indiana, and earned the accreditation of "Canine Behavior Modification Specialist." Andrew Luescher, D.V.M., Ph.D., and Julie Shaw, R.V.T., Animal Behavior Specialist, taught this course. Dr. Luescher and Ms. Shaw are two of the most dedicated dog people I have ever met and I am thrilled that our paths crossed. What I learned in the Dogs course had a profound impact on the way I now teach the Just

House Manners program and is the reason that I just had to rewrite my book. For the past four years, I have been teaching for VCA Animal Hospitals. I have trained hundreds of families with their dogs in the last three years and I am proud to say that over 95 percent of them still have their pets. I also have met some incredible people along the way. Jeanette Floss, D.V.M., M.S., Stephen Hadley, D.V.M., and Stacey Sutphin are three I would like to share with you.

Jeanette Floss not only has become a wonderful friend, but she is one of the most talented and compassionate veterinarians that I have ever met. Her talents are far-reaching when it comes to dealing with her human and animal clients. We have shared several dog behavior-modification clients, and the rewards from working with her would fill another book. Dr. Floss is one of approximately three hundred theriogenologists in the world. (She helps all kinds of animals reproduce.) I am grateful and proud that she agreed to write not only the foreword of this book, but also the chapter on veterinary care—the whats, whys, and whens one needs to know when going to the vet. She's not only caring—her warm sense of humor is evident, too.

I also consider myself very fortunate that my path crossed with that of Dr. Stephen Hadley, Group Vice President for VCA Animal Hospitals. His accomplishments in the field of veterinary medicine reach from coast to coast. He was gracious enough to believe in me and helped spur this book onto successful completion. Stacey Sutphin, VCA's Indiana State Director, gave me a marvelous opportunity when she hired me as the Indiana VCA canine trainer. She believed in my Just House Manners program from the beginning. She has been, and still is, my mentor as well as my good friend. I am blessed to have met these three dog lovers.

Donna Chandler
September 2003

## CHAPTER 1

# Come, Sit —
# and Stay a While

For those of you who did not read my first book, I would like to introduce myself: My name is Donna Chandler, and I have trained dogs and bred them for much of my life. As a matter of fact, I don't ever remember not having or training a dog. I have shown dogs in obedience and confirmation, and I taught dog obedience for fifteen years to 4-H youngsters. I have also owned my own canine obedience school.

It all began when I was eight years old. I got up early one morning to read the want ads in the local newspaper. We didn't have a lot of extra money to spend in our family, but my parents said I could have an "inside dog." All of our dogs up to that point were hunting dogs and were kept outside.

Was it ever my lucky day! An ad in the newspaper read, "Free to good home: border collie, six months old and housebroken." I called right away and spoke to the owner, an elderly woman who was moving in with her son and could not take her dog. This border collie became my prized dog, Mac.

What a friend and companion that border collie turned out to be. Mac and I spent the next seventeen years together—and I do mean together! He went everywhere with me, and by the time I was old enough to have boyfriends they became jealous of all the time I spent with my dog. I loved training him—a talent or sixth sense I seemed to have from the beginning. I began training him the day he came home with me, and he was so very smart. Over the years I taught him more than fifty commands. He was so devoted to me that my mom used to complain about the dirty spot on the wall by the front door of our home—Mac would lie down and wait for me from the time I left for school until I got home.

Mac was a real charmer. One of his really unusual but adorable tricks was when I would say, "Fire," and he would drop to the floor and crawl out of the room. And he loved to protect me: Whenever my parents or my sisters would get upset with me, he would not allow them to come into my room. He never bit anyone; he would just lie at my bedroom door and growl. He had a basket full of toys that included several balls, one of which had a cross symbol on one side of it. You could send him to get his "Christian ball," and out of his six or seven balls he would always pick the one with the cross.

When he was seventeen years old, Mac died of kidney failure. He is buried in Memory Gardens, an animal cemetery in Indianapolis. He was, as my dog-loving friends would say, "An angel—a true angel." I got a new dog right away, although I was sure I would never love any other dog as much as I did Mac. To this day I still think fondly about all the great times he and I had together. My relationship with Mac was the foundation for all I do with animals today.

Of course, I found new dogs to love, train, and appreciate, and am still doing all three of those things today. I learned early on that it is not enough to love and appreciate your dog: he or she must be trained to function in the human world socially. Love and appreciation follow and actually go along with good training. That's what this book is about!

Growing up, I took my dogs to dog shows, where I not only showed them in the obedience rings, but also enjoyed the other animals in the arena and the life at the shows. As my life changed and I married and had children and a career, I had less and less time to spend going to dog shows, but I never stopped training. I married a man who was very involved with horses, and as we travel to horse activities, the dogs always go with us because they are so well-behaved.

Furthermore, when people come to my home, they always comment on how well-mannered my dogs are. They usually say, "Oh, I would have a dog (or still have the one I had) if it behaved like this. How do you do it?" My husband usually responds, "I don't know when she trains them. I rarely see her doing it." Well, folks, it's easy. My training method is very simple. With my busy schedule, my dogs don't go to dog shows but they do go visiting with me because they have Just House Manners. They are welcome wherever we go, and are loved and appreciated because they are so well-mannered. Your dog can be too!

I consider myself not just a dog trainer but also a "dog whisperer." What exactly is "dog whispering"? Whispering is a technique used with many types of animals. Many books have been written about whispering, and the people who wrote those books have different interpretations of its definition. Nevertheless, all the whispering books have a common thread—they teach a positive, loving training method. The main point about whispering that I want you to remember is to communicate using a solid, positive, and loving training plan (like Just House Manners). To me, it means you never set the dog up for failure or use aversive measures in any training.

Dog training methods have changed in the past

five to eight years. Many trainers used to use aversive training methods, harshness, and choke collars, and rarely used food treats as rewards. Today, good trainers use positive reinforcements utilizing verbal and food rewards. Think about it—if someone was aggressive with you, wouldn't you also be aggressive

Prom night was special, and my date waited, patiently and graciously, while I had my picture taken with my beloved Mac.

in return? Most people would, and so would most dogs. The whispering method of dog training eliminates those negative aggressive and aversive responses. Keep in mind that all dogs are food-motivated, and when you add a little love, you have a whispering combination.

During my dog travels, I have met many remarkable people—some of the most wonderful, empathic, and sincere people in the world. "Dog people" are usually that way. Having a love affair with a dog is so rewarding. Truly, there is no other creature that has such sensitive feelings. Your dog accepts all of your moods, your successes and failures, even your bad breath.

Books about dog care and dog training abound on the market these days. But the books about training are often show- or obedience-oriented. What the average dog owner needs is a user-friendly book on day-to-day living happily with a dog. This is that book. You can train your dog by just interacting with him on a daily basis—my method emphasizes that.

So come, sit, and stay a while, and get ready to embark on a great adventure—successful pet ownership.

Little Bear, a Welsh corgi, is a member of my canine family, and has impeccable Just House Manners. However, he is of a breed with natural herding instincts—as he demonstrates here with one of our goats. Before acquiring a new puppy or dog, it is important to do your breed homework and research.

# CHAPTER 2
# Dog Daze

Whenever I visit our local humane society shelters, I frequently see six-month-old to eighteen-month-old unwanted dogs and puppies. The signs on the cages state the reasons for giving up these angels: "NOT HOUSEBROKEN" or "NEEDS ROOM TO RUN" or "MOVING." To me, those words are sad—not valid excuses, but a true copout! They cover up some other truths and are an easy way of saying, "I didn't have a clue on how to train that cute, eight-week-old bundle of fur! It turned into a chewing, unpredictable monster, and I have to get rid of it to keep my sanity or family."

National statistics confirm that 40 percent of all canines purchased or acquired end up in local humane societies, dumped on country roadsides, or in local dog pounds within the first year of their lives. They are canine throwaways of the people who took them into their homes and lives and temporarily gave them their last names. It doesn't need to be this way.

Parents have good motives in the beginning: "The kids wanted a dog and we, the parents, wanted to teach them responsibility." But the novelty wears off quickly. After the first week, when everyone finds out how much work goes with the new, four-legged, member of the family, and you have family members rushing around busy with school, soccer, and baseball practice, the puppy becomes a burden. Nobody wants to take care of it. Then the puppy does something wrong and Dad blames Mom, and Mom blames the kids. Before you know it, the whole household is upset.

The idea that a child can gain responsibility by taking care of a frisky puppy has real drawbacks. Look at it from the dog's point of view—to him, your child is another "puppy," a playmate. A child may not be mature enough to attend to a dog: Would you want an eight-year-old responsible for all of your needs, including feeding you and taking you to the bathroom on a regular basis?

Don't misunderstand. I'd be the last one to say that the children should not be involved in caring for a pet. Of course they should, and it does ultimately teach responsibility. But children should not be the ones totally responsible for the dog you bring into your home. You are, and what is needed is an effective plan. That plan can be implemented in your own home, with the entire family participating.

You don't have to take your dog to an expensive and time-consuming obedience school unless you wish to show him. The average family can train a dog in the home with simple methods that don't take hours. And keep in mind that a dog that is well-behaved in the house is going to be well-behaved outside the house.

I use the term "house manners," and that means just what it says: I think we all want a dog that behaves in the house, doesn't soil the carpet, comes when called, doesn't sniff or jump on guests, and doesn't bark all the time or demand attention. In other words, we want a dog with Just House Manners! That kind of dog stays around.

I recommend that you read this book in its entirety before you embark on the road to canine ownership. It won't take long—I consider it a forty-minute read for a lifetime plan. (Note: If you plan to show your dog, this is not the book for you. You'll need one written specifically on showing dogs.) This book is the short and fairly sweet method to domestic harmony with your pet, not the road to the blue ribbon.

My method utilizes what I call "dog whispering"—it's efficient and simple, demanding only consistency, adherence to the rules, and a true interest in your pet. And most important, there will be no animal shelters or animal control pounds for those who use this book!

# CHAPTER 3

# Let's Get Started!

The first thing you can expect when adopting a dog is major alterations in your lifestyle. Your own family's makeup, home setting, and time availability are all factors to consider when determining which breed of dog to choose.

Choosing the type of dog best for you is as personal as choosing what kind of car, underwear, or a mate is best. The selection requires not only thought, but some research, too. In order to make things easier for everyone concerned, consideration must be given to a number of variables, such as

* Do you want a purebred or a mixed breed?
* Do you prefer big dogs or little dogs?

- How tolerant are you of high energy levels and "mistakes"?
- Are there children in the home, and how old are they?
- What if the dog bites?
- Will shedding fur bother you?
- How old should the canine be when you take him home?
- What about housebreaking and neutering and spaying?
- How much do you know about the basic care and feeding of this little bundle of canine-hood?

There! You know the main questions. Now you need some answers.

### *Should I get a mutt or a purebred?*

I love mixed-breeds, or "mutts." They tend to be about one of the smartest canines known to man because there is no inbreeding. In fact, many of the dogs in show business—in movies or on TV—are mutts. Check them out. There are thousands of them and they come in an endless variety of shapes and sizes. Your local humane society shelter has an availability of hundreds of fine potential pets whose only pedigrees are their good nature, sharp intelligence, and willingness to love everyone in the family—children and adults—if given half a chance and if properly trained.

A visit to the animal shelter can match you with one of these marvelous creatures in exchange for some charges for shots and neutering/spaying. However, if you choose the dog carefully and train him or her correctly, you and your family will be well rewarded. For other sources for finding canine moms with new litters, contact the American Kennel Club, ask your veterinarian for reputable breeders, and check with friends and acquaintances.

## *Size isn't necessarily everything*

I personally love all dog sizes—big, medium, and little—and I've bred and raised all types and like them equally well.

I'll offer some generalizations: Big dogs (around a hundred pounds or more) can adjust very well to living in an apartment or on a farm as long as they have plenty of time with their humans. Therefore, don't base your choice of dog on either its size or that of your home. Instead, base your decision on whether you want a big teddy bear of a pet or a cute little lap puppy, or maybe something in between. However, please be cautious because if you have a physical handicap or are elderly, big dogs can be hard to handle and may even knock you down just because of their size and enthusiasm. On the plus side, whereas most little dogs tend to be excitable and yappy or barky, big dogs lean more toward being mellow and laid-back in personality. Medium-size dogs can go either way—depending on what breed (or breeds) they are—or they can be just right!

Remember, any dog, big or little, can get out of control. Because size and personality are related to breed, you can get specific information regarding characteristics of different breeds from books on dog breeds at the library, from your veterinarian, or from a good pet store. Warning: Although breeders can be very helpful in making a selection, do not call one until you have narrowed your choice of dog with your own book research and a veterinarian. Once you've chosen a breed, find a reputable breeder from whom to buy your puppy. (Again, your vet's office can help you find a good breeder, or contact the American Kennel Club.)

### Will the dog and the kids get along?

If you have young children (seven years old or under), you should check with your local veterinarian for an up-to-date list of breeds that get along well with children and those that are touchier and more prone to biting. Please remember that although there are wonderful and easy-to-get-along-with dogs in every breed, you may not want to play Russian roulette when choosing a new canine member of the family as a companion for your children. Children should have *strict* rules when interacting with either a puppy or adult dog, and any child under the age of seven should always have parental supervision when playing with the canine.

## *The children rules*

- ❧ Children under the age of seven should never be allowed to pick a new puppy up off the ground. If the puppy is dropped, it could be severely hurt or psychologically traumatized permanently. Many puppies that are dropped by children often never like small children when the puppy reaches maturity. I elaborate more on this subject in the "fear period" section of this chapter.

- ❧ Children should not be allowed to lie on the family pet or otherwise treat it like a rug. If a pet is hurt, a defensive bite usually follows. Also, when a child is at eye level, many dogs will interpret that eye level contact as threatening, and that dog is going to defend himself.

- ❧ Adult supervision is absolutely always necessary when a puppy or adult dog first comes into a home with children. All pets should be treated with the utmost respect and not as new toys.

### *What's a little loose fur among friends?*

If you're a picky housekeeper or you have family members with allergies, how much a dog sheds could be a major factor in your selection. Many breeds, particularly curly coated or wirehaired types tend not to shed much. Keep in mind, however, that curly coated and wirehaired dogs do require grooming on a regular basis—whether you do it yourself or have it done by a professional groomer, and you should consider the time and expense involved. Also, remember that regardless of whether you choose a long- or short-haired dog, they all shed, particularly in the spring and fall. And of course, long-haired dogs require more grooming due to their fur matting—another consideration.

Babies and children and puppies can get along in a household if all the "children rules" are followed.

❖   ❖   ❖

## *What age puppy should I get?*

Wherever you get your pup, I suggest that it be nearing eight weeks of age before coming home with you—the young ones still need their mommies. (Puppies go through their first fear period between eight and ten weeks. Fear periods are covered in the following section.) However, I sometimes make an exception to this rule if the pup is of a large breed. Large breeds grow very quickly and can weigh twenty-five to thirty pounds by the time they're eight weeks old.

Puppies develop many distinguishing personality traits by the time they're eight weeks old. When picking a puppy out of a litter, look for a friendly, playful one. When looking for a pet, I recommend not choosing a shy one. You do, however, want a puppy that is submissive and demonstrates a willingness to be a pet.

One test for small-child compatibility is to lay the puppy on its back on the floor and hold it down by rubbing its tummy. If it lies there calmly, that is a good indication that the pup is submissive and will have submissive qualities. However, there is no foolproof test for selecting a new puppy.

Keep in mind, for housebreaking purposes, that most puppies don't have good bladder and bowel control until they're about twelve weeks old.

If you are looking at the pound or humane

society, you will find many dogs, mixed-breed and purebred, that are six months to eighteen months old, which is a great age to begin training. Some of the work has already been done for you just due to the dog's age. Also, you can tell a lot about the dog's personality when the animal is older, so I recommend taking a good look at a slightly older pup.

## *Fear periods*

Puppies go through two fear periods. The first one occurs when they are between eight to ten weeks of age. The second one, which lasts about two weeks, occurs between the ages of four months to twelve months. The first fear period is definite, but the second one can fall randomly between that four- to twelve-month age. During those periods, the part of a dog's brain that registers fear develops, and it evidently applies regardless of breed, whether Great Dane or Maltese or mutt.

If something happens to frighten a puppy during a fear period, it will most likely manifest itself later in the dog's life. For example, as I mentioned earlier, if a child is holding the puppy and drops and hurts him, and the puppy is going through a fear period, it is likely to grow up disliking little children. Or, if a storm rolls through with big lightning flashes and loud thunder that frightens the puppy, he could possibly develop storm fears that will only intensify as he grows older. Therefore, it's important to protect your puppy from serious crises during the first year of his life. (I go into more detail about handling fears later in the book when I discuss whether a dog may need behavior modification.)

### *Habitual behavior*

Dogs (and puppies) learn new behaviors fairly quickly, especially when food and verbal rewards are used. However, behaviors require a minimum of three to four months to become habitual. This is one of the important reasons your dog needs to be on his indoor leash and working on his new behaviors daily.

Let me explain it another way: If you went to China for a week and you couldn't speak the language, you would probably learn several words and phrases, such as "Taxi," "How much?" and so on. Then you would come back home, and within a month or so, you would probably forget almost every word or phrase you had learned. On the other hand, if you were there for three or four months, you would probably never forget the words and phrases you had picked up—they would be embedded in your brain. Compare this to your dog learning your new language. The dog is learning your signals and commands, and within three or four months he will know them and never forget them, or his new behaviors.

## Socializing your newly acquired puppy or adult dog

Teaching your new canine member of the family to get along with humans and other canines is extremely important. The canine should begin being socialized the moment you bring him home.

Your new puppy or dog needs other canine playmates. To find them, you can join a puppy class, go to a dog park, or find an adult dog that is other-dog friendly. The rules are simple:

- ❧ Always have all puppies or dogs on leashes when introducing them to other canines (in case you need to separate them), but drop the leash. Yes, drop the leash. Canines have a friendlier attitude toward each other when they're on their own, with no human hovering at the other end of a leash.

- ❧ At the first sign of any aggression, remove your puppy or dog from the situation. A puppy in a fear period could be permanently traumatized by another dog's aggression, and may not like other dogs when he reaches adulthood. If an aggressive situation arises, find a friendlier canine playmate for your puppy in order to let him know that not all other canines are aggressive.

- ❧ If you want to bring a second adult dog into your home, get a friend to help you out, and find a safe, neutral area (a park, a friend's house—any place but your home) where the dogs can become introduced so your first dog won't feel threatened in his home. Have your friend with the new dog on a leash, while you have your first dog on a leash. Try walking them side by side. If that goes well, try to initiate play with two balls, one for each dog, and progress with play as the dogs feel more comfortable with each other. While playing, drop the leashes. If any aggression occurs, stop play and go back to walking them side by side until all aggression stops. Once the dogs find their comfort zone again, resume playing.

Now that the dogs know each other, you can take them both home, but be sure your first dog is let into the house first. Over the next few weeks, whenever you come into the house, greet your first-owned dog before the second one. This will allow the dominate dog to naturally find his place. Also, let the two dogs play in the yard without your being present as much as possible. By doing this, they won't be protective of you and will be able to find their own level of communication.

❧ If aggression between your dogs becomes a persistent problem, contact a professional trainer or behavior modification specialist immediately.

❧ Always have treats handy for visitors to give your dogs so the pets can get used to—and welcome—people coming into their home.

## What about neutering and spaying?

I firmly believe that all dogs should be neutered (for males) or spayed (for females) unless you plan to breed or show them. This surgery eliminates many unwanted behaviors in both male and female canines without taking the spunkiness out of their personalities.

Dealing with an unspayed female dog in heat (or in season) is a large challenge, a hassle to have to experience, and not necessary if you are not planning to breed your dog. Female canines usually come into heat twice a year for approximately three weeks at a time. They frequently go through frantic personality changes and can become aggressive toward you and anyone else that they come into contact with.

Male canines can smell a female in heat a mile away, so be prepared to have "visitors" at your doorstep. Also be prepared for your female to beat the door down in her efforts to get to her suitors. Male dogs often become very aggressive when a female is near them in heat, and although not all male dogs get worked up then, the majority of them do. In my experience, my male dogs temporarily lose their minds completely.

On the other hand, perhaps the idea of the hassle of a dog in heat doesn't bother you. You have acquired this wonderfully pedigreed dog, and you think you'd like to try your hand at raising a litter of puppies. Be forewarned, and be prepared for the cost associated with breeding and prenatal care of the mom and eight weeks of almost constant care until you sell or find homes for the resulting little darlings. The mother stops—I repeat, stops!—cleaning up after her offspring when they're about three weeks old, or whenever you start supplement feeding them. So, not only will you have puppy piles and puddles everywhere, at the same time you get to take over the three-times-a-day feedings. And puppy food is expensive, as are the first shots and dewormings the puppies will need before they leave their mom for good.

You may have dancing in your head rosy visions of profits made by selling the precious bundles to grateful and responsible dog-owners-to-be. But think about this: What if you don't sell them right away—or ever?

If money to be made by selling puppies is not your reason for not neutering or spaying your dog, but rather you can't afford the procedure, please call your local humane society. They will have a list of area veterinarians who will do the surgery at a discounted cost or for free, depending on your circumstances.

# CANINE PRODUCT LIST

Before you bring your dog home, you need to prepare that home for the new family member—and equipment is vitally important.

Along with a good veterinarian, the must-have items include a crate, a dog bed or rug, a check collar, indoor and outdoor leashes, and hard rubber treat toys. These and other recommendations, as well as important dos and don'ts, are described below.

## CRATES

❖ WIRE CRATE — You most definitely, positively, beyond-a-shadow-of-a-doubt must purchase a crate! The crate should be one of the "denning" spots in your home. The crate needs to be near the family. If you are planning to confine your dog in an out-of-the-way place such as a bathroom, laundry room, or back hallway, then prepare yourself for chewed-up floor moldings, wallpaper, and scratched doors. But when that happens, you have only yourself to blame—not the dog.

American-made wire crates are my favorite (they are very well constructed). They last many years and are easy to maintain, and usually are easy to take down and store. Also, because the wire crate gives the dog a clear

view of his surroundings the dog won't become claus-
trophobic.

You need purchase only one crate for the life of your
dog. The crate should be large enough for your dog to
comfortably stand up and turn around when he or she is
fully grown. However, while your puppy is young and
small, you may want to purchase a "crate divider." Your
trainer can advise you on this subject.

♣ HARD PLASTIC CRATE — A hard plastic, slatted crate
should be used only when traveling. Most airlines require
this type of crate if the dog is going in the cargo hold.

♣ MESH (SOFT) CRATE — These crates are becoming
popular with dog owners. They are great if you are going
to be around the dog during use, thus preventing chews
and possible tumbles. These soft crates are also
excellent for traveling on airplanes if your dog is small
enough to fit under the seat in front of you.

## DOG BEDS OR RUGS

You must have a dog bed or rug. They are crucial in my
training plan. Dog beds come in many shapes, sizes and
colors. I recommend any and all, as long as they have a
cover that can be zipped off and laundered. Most small-
breed dogs like the ones with the sides. If you have an
extremely small-breed pet, you may want to investigate
cat beds. I have several dog beds in my home matching
the color of the room they are in—they do not all have

to look alike. They become your dog's den when he is outside his crate.

### FOOD AND WATER BOWLS

Many types of feeding bowls are on the market these days, from strictly utilitarian to decorative, and this is a personal preference. However, if you have a dog with long ears, you might want to check out food and water bowls designed to keep your dog's ears out of the bowl—a real mess saver. There are also bowls that your dog cannot tip over—great for puppies.

Getting-started essentials—a crate, a dog bed, and sturdy, tip-resistant bowls. Ellie Mae, seen here, began her crate training at eight weeks of age, and by the time this photo was taken at ten weeks, she was already well on her way to having perfect Just House Manners.

It's just as important to keep your pet's dishes as clean as you would your own, so wash the bowls daily. Also, be sure to give your pet clean water every day— twice a day in hot weather.

## COLLARS

❖ CHOKE CHAIN COLLARS are my least favorite training collars. They're often used as a punishing device and people usually use them without the advice of a qualified trainer. A choke chain collar should never be used on a puppy. However, with a trainer's advice, one of these collars can be used for specific exercises. Please be cautious when using them.

❖ CHECK COLLARS are very good for training. They are a continuous-piece nylon collar that slips over the dog's head. The construction is three-fourths nylon, which is adjustable, and one-fourth chain. Check collars are inexpensive and wonderful nonaversive training aids if used properly. They also come in a variety of colors.

❖ ULTIMATE TRAINING COLLARS™ are my personal favorite because they're nonaversive. They're constructed of all nylon, are adjustable, and have a snap closure. The plastic circle where the leash attaches pulls out from the base of the collar when the leash is tugged. (Not all pet supply stores carry this collar, but they are available from Leatherite Nylorite Manufacturing Co. in Lebanon, Indiana. Their phone number is 317-722-5222.)

❖ DECORATIVE COLLARS come in many colors, shapes, and sizes and are made of a variety of materials. They are great if you are experiencing no training problems or your dog has completed all of his/her training.

❖ PINCH COLLARS (also called prong collars) should be used only with advice from a professional canine trainer. These collars are less punishing and harmful than a choker and can be very effective. They give a pinch instead of a choke if used properly. These collars have saved many a dog from being surrendered to a shelter.

❖ GENTLE LEADERS—my personal choice—are a type of head halter collar that is more expensive than all the other head halters on the market. However, they are well worth the investment and are my very favorite of all of the head halters that are available. If you are going to use a head halter, then purchase an instructional video with it or get advice from a professional trainer. Many trainers (including myself) and pet owners love this type of collar and will be more than happy to assist you with your selection.

### INDOOR LEASH

This is one of my key training secrets. An indoor leash is any four- to five-foot nylon leash with a lightweight buckle that attaches to the collar. Many people who have puppies or small breeds use cat leashes. The indoor leash is what "dog whispering" is all about—setting the dog up for success, not failure. Don't be home without one.

### Outdoor leash

The outdoor leash should be at least six feet long (so training can take place while you are walking your dog) and can be made of your choice of leather, nylon, or cloth—but not chain.

### Retractable leash

I love retractable leashes *only* after your dog is trained to walk down the street without pulling you. They also come in really handy if this is the only way you can exercise your dog or if you are traveling and need to stop for a potty break.

### Canine seat belts

Canine seat belts are available on the market and are relatively inexpensive. They come in many sizes and are good for traveling with your pet. I will talk more about this product in the section on traveling with your pet.

### Tie-out cables

Tie-out cables can be very handy if used properly. The following are a couple of circumstances where I recommend the use of tie-out cables:

* If you don't have a fenced-in yard and this is the only way for the dog to be out and lie in the sun once in a while.
* If you don't leave your dog out all day or all night on a tie-out cable.

    Remember—your dog has your last name and needs

to be inside with his family. Chaining a dog outside alone for long periods of time can create stress and result in an aggressive dog.

♣    ♣    ♣

##  Food-oriented rewards

Food-oriented rewards are easy to use and are a must when teaching your dog a new behavior. All dogs are food motivated—a dog that doesn't take a treat is a stressed dog. Treats should be desirable and in very tiny pieces—no bigger than your little fingernail—so that it is a morsel reward, not a meal. If you wish to use dog bones, then put them in a plastic bag and hammer away

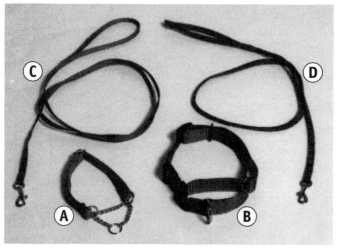

I prefer nonaversive collars, such as the part-nylon, part-chain check collar (A), and my favorite, the all-nylon Ulitmate Training Collar (B). A sturdy outdoor leash (C), about 6 feet long, is vital; but just as important is a 4- to 5-foot-long indoor leash (D)—one of the key secrets to successfully teaching Just House Manners.

to break them up. It also helps to change the treat often—plain Cheerios and even ice cubes are good choices, and some dogs like vegetables and garlic.

When teaching a new behavior, reward each and every correct response. The food treats should be wherever your puppy is going to be while he is going through training. I keep them all over the house in plastic containers with lids. The important thing to remember is that treats should be immediately available whenever your dog does an appropriate behavior. You have only two—*two!*—seconds to reward your dog for good behavior in order for him or her to make the connection.

### TREAT BAGS

Treat bags that you clip on your belt or pants are available at most pet stores. (If you're creative, you can make them, or you can even use a fanny pack.) These bags are very handy while training. Also, while your dog is in training, always consider your walk times training times. It helps to have a treat bag hanging with your outdoor leashes so the treats are readily available any time you go for a walk.

### VOICE

Your voice can be your best asset—and it's free. Be consistent with your "command" voice and your "loving" voice so your dog will know the difference. I refer to my command voice as the "God-to-Moses" voice. If God talked, wouldn't you listen? Rather than a harsh voice, the command voice is more of an attention-getter.

## CLICKERS

A clicker is a little device you hold in your hand, and it is a marvelous way to train by conditioning a dog to respond. Several articles have been written on the benefits of clicker training (several by Julie Shaw of Purdue University), and classes and books are available. I highly recommend this type of training as very effective; however you must be very dedicated, and this method requires more time than the Just House Manners plan.

## ELECTRIC SHOCK PRODUCTS

❖ ELECTRIC FENCES are a wonderful invention, especially with neighborhood ordinances and limited budgets. However, always remember that some dogs can break through them, and they don't keep other dogs or predators from getting to your pet. They don't stop people either—your wonderfully trained pet can be stolen. A regular fence is my personal favorite, but if that's not in your budget, opt for the electric fence.

❖ ELECTRIC BARKING SHOCK COLLARS can be a very effective tool if it works properly (inexpensive models usually do not work consistently). Because they cause discomfort and can even be painful to the canine, these collars should be used only if all other training methods truly have been exhausted.

❖ SCAT MATS are mats with a cord that you plug into the wall, and it's usually used to keep a dog off the furniture. It's a good training aid as long as you use it consistently.

♣ ELECTRONIC TRAINING COLLARS are expensive (many companies make them) and should be used only with expert advice from an animal behaviorist or qualified trainer, and only if your only other consideration is euthanasia. Please research all other conventional training methods first.

### HOUSEBREAKING BELLS

These bells are an inexpensive and terrific housebreaking aid—I believe they are an absolute necessity when housebreaking your dog. The bells—two or more—are fastened to a cord which is attached to a suction cup. Stick the cup at a level where the dog can reach the bells on the door he goes out to do potties. Before long, the dog learns that every time the bells ring, the door opens—classic conditioning. I have yet to have a dog or new puppy that didn't learn this trick within two to three weeks.

The suction cup allows you to move the bells up and down the door as your pet grows, and the bells don't get caught in the door when it opens and closes. However, the suction cup may not stick to a wooden door, in which case you may have to attach them to the door knob. This can be a little bit of a hassle in opening and closing the door, but your pet will not fail at letting you know when he needs to go outside.

## Neutralizing deodorizers

Products that neutralize odors (there are many on the market) are a must to have around in case your new puppy has an accident. Always clean the accident spot thoroughly and then spray with a neutralizing deodorizer. This "unmarks" the area, and the puppy is unlikely to return to that spot to do his business again.

## Dog toys

❖ HARD RUBBER TREAT TOYS — You *must* purchase at least a couple of hard rubber treat toys. (I personally have one for each of my dogs for each day of the week.) These are among the greatest toy/training tools on the market, and are available under many brand names, such as "Kong," "Treat Ball," or "Power Chew." These toys come in different sizes so you can purchase the right size for your canine. They are dishwasher safe, and you'll use them throughout the dog's life.

❖ RAWHIDES — It's hard for me to resist the toy section when I visit a pet supply store. Canines of all ages just love the rawhide chew toys—bones, pig ears, and so on. Just be sure to purchase rawhide products that fit the size of your pet.

❖ NYLON BONES — If you have a puppy that is teething, I recommend these hard nylon chew bones. They are very good for all breeds that are chewers (although most breeds do chew to some extent) and come in several sizes and flavors to accommodate various dog sizes and tastes.

The really heavy chewing period usually starts when the pup is very young and lasts until he or she is twenty-four to thirty months old. One of the reasons nylon bones are among my favorite dog toys is because they last longer than rawhides. However, I recommend that you purchase both a few rawhide chew bones as well as nylon bones.

♣ STUFFED ANIMAL TOYS — The stuffed animal toy department is filled with many different stuffed toys—dogs love them and they are easy to clean.

Remember, chewing is normal for dogs, so don't worry if your dog shreds this type of toy.

♣ ROPE TOYS — Rope toys are great for dog-and-dog play. This toy can create an urge to play tug-of-war, which for dogs is power play. Tug-of-war teaches a dog to bite; therefore, rope toys should be forbidden for human-and-dog play. However, two dogs can play tug-of-war with no aggressive consequences.

♣ TENNIS BALLS — A must in the dog toy department, tennis balls for dogs also come in many sizes now so you can choose the right size for your dog. Also available are tennis balls attached to floating ropes if you have a water dog (such as a retriever) or live on or visit a lake.

♣ SQUEAKER TOYS — Most dogs love squeaker toys, but I must caution you that the squeaker devices can be chewed out and swallowed. If one gets caught in the dog's digestive system, your pet will have to undergo pricey emergency surgery that could also cost the life of the pet. Don't forbid squeaker toys, but let your dog play with them only under supervision, and put them away when you are done.

🐾    🐾    🐾

## Potty training aids

🐾 PIDDLE (OR POTTY) PADS — Piddle or potty pads are great tools for people who live in high-rise apartments, elderly people who can't go outside in bad weather, very small dogs (many of the toy breeds) who cannot handle the outside elements, or the occasional breed that for some reason just cannot be housebroken. The pads (there are several kinds to choose from) have a dog-potty scent that dogs can smell but you can't. This encourages the dog to use the pad as dogs like to "mark their territory" by going potty over another dog's potty.

Potty pads can be placed by the back door or in the garage, and you can take your dog there to do his business, and the pads make for an easy clean-up.

You still can train your dog to go outside to do his business, but for "thin-skinned" or toy breed dogs who are sensitive to the cold, you may want to place potty pads in the garage during the really bad winter months.

🐾 LITTER BOXES — These are not just for cats! They are effective and useful, and like potty pads, litter boxes can often be used for puppies, dogs who live in high-rise apartments, dogs with elderly owners, and during inclement weather.

## Dog clothing

Dog clothing comes in many styles and colors for all seasons. Have fun and dress your baby up. Many dogs almost need a closet for all their clothes. The kids also have fun with Halloween and Christmas costumes.

## Travel kits

Travel kits are available in some pet stores. You can buy one already made up or you can make your own. A good hard plastic case with the essential dog products is a good idea if you are traveling with your pet. Bottled water and your dog's own food is good idea (it frequently prevents diarrhea). Having a travel kit put together will eliminate forgetting valuable, necessary items when you are traveling. By the way, there are many hotels and resorts that will accommodate you and your pet. After reading this book and following the Just House Manners plan your dog is going to be so well mannered that you can take him almost anywhere!

# CHAPTER 4

# Let's Bring Your New Puppy or Dog Home!

Now you have your list of must-haves. If you can't afford these items, such as a crate, check collar or Ultimate Training Collar, and indoor and outdoor leashes, along with the other items mentioned, you probably can't afford the dog.

Before you get your puppy or dog, you should already have bought these necessary supplies, which will make life for you and your pet easy and well-organized. The packing has been removed, any necessary assembly has been done, and the items have been placed in the areas of your home where you've decided your pet will be allowed to go. Now you're ready to pick up your new family member and bring him or her home.

Reminder Number One (and never forget this): English is not your canine's first language—he does not understand it. Now, having made that clear, during the car ride home after you pick your pet up, talk to him any way you like, calling him a cute baby and so forth (you know—the baby-talk gibberish). Not only will your talking be reassuring to the dog as he enters a new and probably frightening environment, it will accustom him to your voice.

This "small talk" has an added bonus: Even though your dog's training has not yet begun, the more you talk to him the sooner he'll learn to recognize the difference between your loving voice and your command voice.

♣   ♣   ♣

## Crate placement

For the first couple of weeks your dog's crate should be placed in a convenient place where your family spends most of its time, such as the kitchen. Not only does this allow your pet to see his new family all the time, but it also to allows the dog to feel secure about being in the crate.

Please, don't ever put the crate in the basement! Think about it—would you like to be locked in a dark room, far away from everyone? If you worry about how the crate looks in the room or how much space it takes up, keep in mind that it will be in this spot only temporarily. You'll keep the crate in the family area only until your puppy feels comfortable in the crate and doesn't whine any more, probably only a short time. Then you can move the crate to a space that's more convenient for you, such as the back hall or laundry room (as long as these places aren't dark).

Rub an old blanket, towel, flannel shirt (my favorite item), or T-shirt—anything soft—all over you and other family members' arms and faces to personalize it with your scents. Then place it in the crate for your new dog to cuddle with. (If you use an item with buttons, be sure to cut the buttons off to prevent your dog from chewing and possibly eating something that could be harmful.) This item will become a source of security for your new canine as he acquaints himself with your scents. Most dogs can remember up to fifty different smells. Those of you and your family should, of course, be your dog's most cherished scents, and the sooner he gets used to them the better. If he soils on this (or any other bedding you put in his crate), remove the item, wash and rescent it and cut it into strips, then tie the strips inside the crate. If he still soils his bed, remove the bed until he no longer is soiling in his crate.

There is a crate "golden rule" that I must emphasize: Never talk to your dog while he is in his crate—never!—even when he's a puppy. Talking to him only increases anxiety and will increase the chances of your dog developing separation anxiety (remember the fear periods). Separation anxiety is manifested by the dog constantly drooling, barking, or biting himself, or otherwise indulging in other bad habits. Many dogs with separation anxiety have to take medication and go through behavior modification with a veterinarian and canine trainer. So avoid this and just leave your dog alone and never talk to him while he is in his crate.

Say, for example, your dog is in his crate, barking constantly, and you know that it is only to get attention. So you go to him in his crate and say, "No bark, be quiet," and the dog keeps barking. The dog is getting what he wants—your attention. He doesn't care if it is negative or positive, as long as he is getting attention. On the other hand, if you ignore him, he'll soon learn that his crate time is quiet time and the barking will stop.

Your eight- to fourteen-week-old puppy's first few nights at home should be get-acquainted nights, with lots of love and petting and no training except for teaching him to sleep and be in his crate. However, if you acquire an older dog (five months and older) you can jump right into training after only a couple of nights.

## Housebreaking
### using the crate, the indoor leash, and hard rubber treat toys

It is my belief that every canine can easily be housebroken—and the crate is one of the keys to success! The other trick to successful housebreaking is the indoor leash (more about this later). The crate and the indoor leash must be used in combination. Whenever your dog or puppy is out of his crate he must be on his indoor leash and be with a responsible member of the family. He is not safe anywhere in your home until he has some training and his chewing days are over.

Canines have a natural instinct for denning. From the beginning, wild dogs and their ancestors lived in dens, big enough only to stand up and turn around in. Your modern-day domestic dog still has that instinct to create a small, secure space for himself, and his crate will become that place if he is properly trained. Therefore, instead of thinking that a crate is cruel, think of it as providing your canine with his own "space"—like you and your favorite chair.

Also, by the time dogs reach three months of age, bladder and bowel control kicks in and they are unlikely to ever do potties in their den. (Unlike human children, this instinct is inborn with canines.)

Now, go back and read the previous paragraph again, then keep this item in mind: For the first two or three nights, you should place a double or triple thickness of newspaper in the front part of the crate. This is the most likely place he will do his business until bladder and bowel control kicks in, and the extra thickness of paper provides easy clean up.

Once your canine has had two clean nights in a row, don't put paper in the crate any more. You will have been taking your dog outside frequently for his "business trips" so he'll learn that is where he is supposed to go.

You also should feed your canine in his crate; this helps him to like his crate and further discourages him from messing there. However, never leave his water in his crate overnight. All he will do is drink and tinkle—especially in the beginning.

If you work outside the home, your canine can probably stay in his crate for up to eight hours, but keep your dog's age in mind regarding his bladder and bowel control. Try to come home at your lunch break to let or take the dog outside, especially in the beginning when he is very young. If you are going to be gone for more than four hours, leave about one-third of a bowl full (preferable a tip-proof bowl) of water in his crate. Would you want to be left alone without a drink of water all day?

Whenever you put the dog in his crate, use a command, such as "Kennel up." (You can use any command but be consistent.) He will learn the association and will eventually go to his crate on his own when he hears your command. This is the time to give him a hard rubber treat toy stuffed with a goody. The only time your pet should ever get one of these toys is when he's in his crate (not at bedtime) and you're going to be gone for a period of time, or you're busy and need free time away from the dog. I like to prepare my week's worth of peanut butter-stuffed hard rubber treat toys on Sunday evening;

that way I have peanut butter on my hands—and under my fingernails—only once a week.

I stuff treat toys three-fourths full with peanut butter, then put them in a large storage bag and put them in the freezer. When I give these treats to the dogs frozen it takes them twice as long to get the peanut butter out. This provides *great* entertainment for your dog while you're out, and by the time he's finished with his hard rubber treat toy he will need a nap to recover from all the energy he has exerted. Then you can take the empty hard rubber treat toy and just put it in the dishwasher. Believe me—the hard rubber treat toy is your dog's best friend whenever you're not at home and he's alone.

When you're planning to go out, give the "kennel up" command about fifteen minutes before you leave, put your dog in his crate, give him a hard rubber treat toy, avoid eye contact with him, and leave. And remember the crate golden rule: Don't talk to him. Don't explain, "Your family is leaving and we'll be back soon." And when you return, don't say anything like, "Your family is home, we're coming to get you." Don't talk to him at all. Just walk past the dog without saying a word or making eye contact with him, put your things down, change your clothes or shoes, and get ready to go for a walk. The coming-home process shouldn't take more than ten minutes, and once you're ready, go let your dog out of his crate. *Then* talk all that "I missed you" talk.

To summarize, the crate and hard rubber treat toy

are two key secrets to successful housebreaking, because when the dog is in his crate and happy with a hard rubber treat toy, he won't foul his own den. First, your dog learns not to potty in his crate; eventually he learns that the whole house is his den, and he won't potty anywhere in the house. Likewise, he'll quickly learn that when he's let out of his crate, he's immediately taken to where he can do his business. This arrangement should leave no opportunity for accidents on your floor. (However, if an accident does occur, remember to use a neutralizing deodorant product to help avoid any future accidents in the same spot.)

All dogs should be walked daily, regardless of the size of your yard. Make it a family time, and work on all your commands while out for the walk. Remember to take your treat bag with food rewards with you.

♣     ♣     ♣

### When does your dog have to go potty?

Dogs aren't much different from humans. And if you use the following five "golden rules," you should have a housebroken dog in no time.

Take a dog out to go potty:

- ♣ Whenever you take him out of his crate.

- ♣ After he eats, within a twenty- to thirty-minute time frame.

- ♣ After he has had a vigorous playtime. If you play with him outdoors, take him to his potty spot before bringing him in the house. If you play with him indoors, take him out promptly when you're finished. (Think about how you feel and what *you* have to do after you've had a good workout.)

- ♣ Anytime he wakes up from a nap. What's the first thing you do when you wake up from sleep?

- ♣ Right before you retire him to his kennel at night.

♣     ♣     ♣

### Some crate dos and don'ts

I have emphasized that when you're not with your canine, he should always be in his crate. This should be an absolute rule until he is two years old. I have also stressed that you should never talk to your dog while he is in his crate.

Just as important, your dog should never be left outside, even in a fenced-in yard, for the day. Some people think not leaving a dog outside is cruel. However, even though the dog may not be able to get out of the yard, remember that until he is two years old—I repeat, *two years old*—he will be in his heavy chewing stage and will probably chew up everything in sight: the lawn furniture, the picnic table, your children's toys, the side of the house, anything he can sink his sharp little teeth into. Furthermore, there is nothing to guarantee that he won't jump the fence or dig his way out, which puts him at risk for a whole other set of problems, such as being hit by a car.

Just in case I'm not making myself perfectly clear, the plan is that you will have this canine until death do you part, and hopefully, that death won't be premature.

There are, nonetheless, a few exceptions to the crating rules. For example, if your dog whines during the first few nights in his crate (and believe me, he will), go to him, give him some loving, and take him outside—he just might have to go. Then put him back in his crate and leave him. If he is a young puppy, you may need to have the crate by your bed the first few nights (everyone needs their sleep) until he is comfortable with his new surroundings. During the day move his crate to the location you have chosen for when he is older.

You need never feel guilty about using a crate, because as I said before, because of their instinctive denning needs, dogs tend to like crates. But if you mistreat your dog or use the crate for punishment, the effect will be quite the opposite. Used properly, your dog will probably go cheerfully into his crate on his own.

### Housebreaking using housebreaking bells

First thing in the morning—yes, before you shower or have that first cup of coffee or do anything else!—go to your dog, clip on his outdoor leash (before letting him out of his crate), and promptly take him outside. While you're walking him to the door grab a food treat, call him by name, and say, "Outside." Ring the housebreaking bells (which should be hung on the door as described earlier in the book), but don't talk or say anything about the bells—just ring the bells and take the dog outside. By doing this, almost all dogs—99.9 percent of them—learn within two weeks to ring the bells whenever they want to go outside. It's one of those classic conditioned responses: The dog knows that every time those bells ring, that door opens.

Housebreaking bells are a marvelous tool that can

even be taken with you when you travel. Remember, a dog that is housebroken at home is not always housebroken in someone else's home. Take his bells with you when you travel and let the dog see you hang them on the door. The dog will then figure, "There are my bells and that must be the door where I go out to do my potty."

When you take your dog outside, always take him to where you want him to potty—the same spot every time. In time all you'll need to do is stand at the door and he'll automatically go to where he's supposed to potty.

After he's done his business, tell him what a good dog he is and give him a treat (remember—you have only two seconds to reward him). Take him back into the house, put him back into his crate, and feed him. Now you can take care of your own business—workout, get the kids off to school, or get ready for work. However, because eating stimulates the dog's bowels, take him outside to do his business once more before you leave the house. This should be within a twenty- to thirty-minute period after you feed him. This also gives you time to interact with your dog.

If you are alert and aware of your dog's natural needs—remember the five rules of knowing when your dog has to go potty—and use the crate, the indoor and outdoor leashes, and housebreaking bells, you won't have any housebreaking problems.

However, using effective housebreaking methods

and tools doesn't mean there won't be any accidents at all. If an accident does happen, say the dog's name and take him outside to his potty spot. (Your initial reaction may be to say "No, no!" to your dog. However, that will make only you feel better; it will likely mean nothing to your dog.) Even if he doesn't potty at that time, tell him he is a good dog, give him a food treat, and bring him back inside. Keep in mind that this has to happen immediately after the accident for your dog to make the correct association. Also remember the three to four months needed to establish habitual behavior, so be consistent.

Do not—I repeat, *do not!*—ever hit or spank your dog. That won't housebreak him, but consistent use of the crate and responsible training will teach him desirable behavior.

Most of my dogs have had one or two accidents in the house, almost always when they were very young. You, too, will probably have to accept a couple of accidents as part of the price for the pleasure your dog will give you.

Some dogs never "break training"—good luck on finding one of those rare breeds! But soon your dog will be well behaved, and you'll be proud of him and yourself. Your canine should be well on his way to being housebroken within two to four weeks, and possibly sooner if he is more than three months old.

### All-around-the-house-breaking

Housebreaking your dog to places in the house where he has never been is a short but essential part of his training. Perhaps you've discovered your dog somewhere new, say at the top of the stairs, and you could tell by the guilty look on his face that he's just done something naughty—like pottying upstairs. He probably thought he could hide it. After all, there weren't any witnesses, right? No one saw him. Furthermore, because he hasn't been allowed upstairs, he thinks no one lives up there.

The solution to this problem is simple. When your dog is about eighteen months old and doing well with all his training and is responding to the "on your rug" command (described later in the book), put his rug in your bedroom at bedtime. Shut the bedroom door, say, "On your rug—down, stay." I can almost guarantee that 99.9 percent of the time he will still be on that rug when you wake up in the morning.

You have already conditioned your dog to consider the crate his den, and remember, dogs don't potty in their dens. After a couple of days of his sleeping on his rug in the new environment, your worries will be over. That part of the house (and in time, the rest of the house) will have become part of his life, and his den, and he won't potty there anymore.

You may have to spend some time in several

rooms before he gets the idea that he can't potty in those rooms. Take a blanket or towel or his rug to a room he previously hasn't been allowed in. Give him the "on your rug—down, stay" command, and just hang out with him in that room for a short time, reading, working on the computer, and so on. The dog will think, "Oh, I live in here too. This is a part of my den, and I don't potty in my den." There you go—now he is on his way to becoming housebroken to the entire house.

If he does still have an occasional accident, it's probably because he was too young and not ready to be out of his crate without supervision for any length of time. Return to beginning training for a while, and I'm confident that you will be off and running with success in no time.

# CHAPTER 5

# Giving Effective Commands and Training With "Dog Whispering"

### *The "God to Moses" voice*

If God talked to you, wouldn't you listen? Most people would, and that is what you want to have in mind when you want to give a good, firm command. Keeping your voice low and firm, say the dog's name, then the command. When he obeys, follow up by using your loving voice and offering a treat. Remember, your dog doesn't know English, so you are teaching him a new language and you want to be sure he hears it. Your voice is a valuable asset in training, and it's free.

### Using the indoor leash and the "Come" and "Sit" commands

**[1 exercise — 2 commands]**

"Come" is the Number One command for a dog to learn. Nothing is more frustrating to a dog owner than calling a dog and having it not come. This can also be dangerous for the pet if he slips his collar and there is a busy street or other hazard nearby.

One of the most effective aids for teaching a dog to come is the indoor leash. In fact, along with the crate, the indoor leash is one of the key secrets for any successful dog training, and one of the secrets to dog whispering—you have more control and thus are never setting the dog up for failure.

Beginning the second or third day after bringing your new dog home, you should start keeping him on a leash while he's in the house. That's right, in the house—hence the term "indoor leash." Whenever your dog is not in his crate, he should wear an indoor leash for the first four to six months of his new life with you, regardless of his age at the time you acquired him. However, if the dog is older and already knows some commands, you may be able to cut the indoor-leash time to around four months.

The dog will probably resist the leash in the beginning, but keep at it. At first let him drag the leash around while you're right there with him. He may be frightened of it, but he will get used to it. After a while, pick up the leash, call his name and say, "Come," in a command voice. Give the leash a gentle little tug and try to pull him to you. Keep saying "come" until he comes to you, and when he arrives, tell him to sit while slightly pulling up on his collar and pushing down on his rump. When he obeys, give him lots of love and a tiny treat. (Remember—you have only two seconds to give the food reward for your dog to make the connection.) Go through this process fifteen or so times a day. Have the entire family join in. Everyone should take turns picking up the leash and saying the dog's name, then, "Come, sit," and giving him his reward verbally and with a treat.

When you are first training your dog, you may want to use an encouraging and loving "come" command as well as the God-to-Moses "come" command to lure him to you, then command him to sit, with the immediate follow-up of verbal and treat rewards. One bonus of making him sit every time he comes to you is that it will keep him from jumping on you in the future. He'll soon learn that when he comes he must sit before he receives a reward and your attention. In no time at all, he'll learn to come and sit at your command, and then be happily rewarded by big hugs and lots of love from you. Eventually you'll need to give only verbal rewards and not a food treat. (Note: Keep in mind that whenever you start teaching your dog a new command, always use a food treat until the dog has solidly learned the command, about ninety days.)

The "come" command can be taught indoors and out. Pick up the leash (indoor or outdoor) and tell the dog to "come" and "sit." Then give him a food treat and a verbal reward. Repeat this process anywhere from fifteen to twenty times a day until the dog has learned the command.

You may not accomplish great results the first night of indoor-leash training, but by the third or fourth day you should be well on your way. This technique is also very effective in teaching your dog how to walk on a leash, whether indoors or outdoors. When you're outdoors for a walk, and the dog starts to pull or tug on the leash, stop, call the dog, say, "Come, sit," and reward him. Repeat this as many times as necessary until he stops pulling and tugging. This training will ensure that your dog will walk comfortably with you in the future. This is also why I never use retractable leashes until a dog is trained. You may have to reassure him from time to time that this big, unknown leash is not a monster, but it will be worth it.

A word of caution: Don't ever leave the leash on the dog when he's in his crate—it could become tangled and choke him, or he might chew it up, and then you'll have to buy another one.

Using the indoor leash enables your dog to spend more time with you and the family outside of his crate. Keep the leash on your dog when he's lying on his rug by your chair while you read or watch TV. While you cook dinner, attach the leash to your belt so he can be out in the kitchen with you. By using the indoor leash this way, you'll know where your dog is at all times, and he won't be chewing up *your* "toys," such as antique chairs or your brand-new shoes.

If your children want to have the dog nearby

Spending as much time as possible with their humans helps dogs learn to socialize much better than when left alone. Keep the indoor leash on your dog while you read or watch TV so he can enjoy your company outside of his crate.

And while you cook or clean up the dinner dishes, attach the leash to your belt so your dog can be in the kitchen with you.

while they watch TV, or just want to play with him, make sure they also keep his leash on.

Remember also that when your children have been playing with the dog for a while—and with kids, the play has probably been pretty vigorous— he'll probably have to go potty, so take him out right away. You'll really be glad for the indoor leash then, because your dog will literally be at your command and you can ward off potential accidents. (When you take your canine outside he should always be on his leash, unless he's in a fenced-in yard or until you are very confident that he will always come to you when he's called.)

When the four- to-six-month training period is over and you have removed the leash, if your dog starts forgetting his commands, put his indoor leash back on for two to three days for a refresher course— it's so easy. The indoor leash is a valuable tool when introducing any dog to a new home, and you'll want to use short refresher courses with it if you move or take your dog with you when you travel. If you take your dog visiting, keep him on his indoor leash while in your friend's home; he can't get into mischief and I'm sure he'll be invited back. You'll soon discover that the indoor leash, along with the crate, will become one of your best training tools! You'll never have anything chewed up, and you'll always know where your dog is.

## *"Leave it" and "Take"*

### [1 exercise — 2 commands]

"Leave it" is a command that you will use whenever you do not want your dog to have something or he is behaving in a way you don't approve of, such as chewing on anything that does not belong to him, reaching for food, shoelaces, digging in your garden, and so on. Use the "leave it" command instead of the word "no," which means nothing to the dog unless you attach it exclusively to a specific behavior.

This is a very simple command and is taught by simply giving your dog a treat. With leash in hand, ask your dog if he wants a treat. (Whatever you call it, whether a "goodie" or "cookie," just be consistent.) Hold the treat near his mouth and say, "Leave it," while giving him a slight tug on his collar and pulling him back from the treat. Repeat this process several times until he no longer goes after the treat. Then offer him the treat while saying "Take," and give him the treat along with a verbal reward. Repeat this exercise four to five times daily.

This command will come in handy both in the house and outside. For example, if you are out for a walk in the park with the dog is off leash and he gets into the scrubby grass or goes chasing off after a squirrel, all you have to say is "Leave it" and "Come." The dog will drop what he is doing and come. You will love this command because it prevents or stops negative behavior. It also teaches him not to take anything out of your hands without the "take" command, and he will soon learn that he can have food from your hand only with the "take" command.

♣　　♣　　♣

## *"On your rug—down, stay"*
### [1 exercise — 3 commands]

The dog rug or dog bed is one of the primary must-have pieces of equipment mentioned in the first chapter, and ideally you will have been using it from the very moment you brought your puppy home (but never in the crate). And another one of the great training secrets is the "on your rug—down, stay" command—one of the few phrase commands you'll teach your dog.

You can teach this command while you're reading, working on the computer, doing homework, or any time you are idle. But one of the best times is while you're watching televison.

There are approximately twenty minutes of commercial time per hour of TV programming, during which you can either train your puppy or dog or you can pop up to go to the refrigerator for a snack. If you use that time to train your canine, you might even lose a few pounds—an added bonus! (But keep your favorite TV beverage handy so you won't feel too deprived.)

Place the rug about two to three feet away from

you. During a commercial, guide your dog (attached to his indoor leash, of course) onto the rug and tell him, "On your rug—down, stay." From the dog's sitting position, gently push him into the down position while giving a gentle tug on his collar and repeating the "down" command. Then put your hand in front of his nose and say, "Stay." Give him a chew bone to keep him occupied, then go back and sit in your chair. He will probably get up and come to you, but just pick up his leash, take him back to the rug, and repeat the commands. Somewhere between the tenth to fifteenth time he'll begin to stay put.

Each time you do this, it will take less and less time to get him to stay on his rug. After the dog has caught on to the concept, begin to leave him on his rug for longer periods, say for about ten minutes. Then tell him, "Come, sit," and praise and food treat him. Then repeat the "on your rug" training. Your goal is to get him to stay on his rug from one commercial break to the next, and in time, for a full one-hour TV program.

He may not master the "down, stay" command right away, but he will shortly. Furthermore, he won't be confused if you teach him more than one command at a time. So call him by name and then in your firm God-to-Moses voice say, "On your rug—down, stay."

It will also be helpful to put his favorite toys on his rug. This is where your dog will stay while you are reading or watching TV or are otherwise involved.

Your dog will come to love his rug; you'll be able to move the rug around the house as circumstances require, and he will always know what to do whenever you give the command.

The rug will become your dog's own space very soon after this training begins, and after you no longer use the crate and remove it (when he's about two and a half years old). His rug will replace the crate, providing security and his special denning spot. You might even consider buying more than one rug. I have four rugs in my home: one in the family room, one in my office, one in my bedroom, and one in the back hall where the crate used to be.

Remember, your dog will be learning your language commands during the four- to six-month training period. Therefore, the indoor leash is a must during this period. Always be firm and consistent with the command, as the ability to stay put is vital to your dog's good indoor behavior. You will use this exercise when he rings the housebreaking bells and you know he doesn't have to go outside, when you are eating dinner, or in your family room watching a movie. Just imagine you have guests and your dog is happily extending a typical dog welcome: sniffing, licking, maybe jumping. Now imagine that all you have to do is call him by name and say, "On your rug—down, stay." Trust me, your guests will be very pleased (and impressed!) not to have your dog jumping head to toe, all over their good clothes.

My own dogs are on the rug whenever we have

guests, and they aren't allowed off unless they're called. All my guests are amazed—and grateful!—at how well-behaved my dogs are in the house. Even though I am myself a dyed-in-the-fur dog lover, when I go to visit someone, the last thing I want is for the family dog to jump, drool, romp, or push me down—not to mention being snuffled in a human's most intimate and embarrassing places.

❖   ❖   ❖

## *A few more ways to work with the "stay," "down," and "sit" commands*

### "Stay"

The "stay" command can be taught at any time: while you're watching TV (beverage in place—we don't want our training sessions interrupted), or while you're out for a stroll. Tell your dog to sit. Holding the leash, face the dog and back up in front of him while holding the hand without the leash in front of his nose, simultaneously calling him by name and saying, "Sit—stay, stay." If he gets up, repeat the steps until you can take two or three steps backward and he stays. Repeat this exercise often regardless of where you are.

Each time you tell your dog to sit and stay and he actually stays, reward him with a treat, big hugs, and love. Before long, you'll be able walk into another room and he will stay where you put him. And, as

Teach your dog to "stay" by holding his leash in front of him. Back away from the dog while calling him by name and saying "Sit, stay." After he stays for a short period, tell him to "come" and "sit," then give him a food and verbal reward. Repeat these steps as often as needed. The "stay" command is also used with the "on your rug—down, stay" command.

with all commands, when teaching this one, remember to always use your stern (but loving) God-to-Moses voice.

❖

### "Down"

You can also work on the "down" command at any time. When teaching this command, you must always have your dog in a sitting position first. With one hand, grasp his leash where it attaches to his check collar, and place your other hand on the dog's shoulders. Give a gentle tug downward on the leash and gently but firmly push down on the dog's shoulders while calling him by name and saying, "Down, down." If your dog remains sitting, or raises his rump, start over again from the beginning, with the dog in the sitting position. Once you get him down give the command, "Down, stay." Repeat the command several times. You can also try to lure him down (from a sitting position) with a treat. With the dog in a sitting position, tell him "Down" while holding the food treat down low and slowly pulling it away from the dog. Keep repeating the "down" command and when he is down say, "Stay."

If he rolls over onto his back, just ignore it; he may want his tummy rubbed, but that isn't part of this lesson. In time he'll go down in a normal dog position.

Remember to give him lots of love after each

To teach a dog "down," first make sure he's in a sitting position. Give a slight tug on the leash while pushing on his shoulders and repeatedly saying, "Down." You can also lure the dog down with food treats. The key is to be sure he's in a sitting position first.

short session. Your canine should master the "down" command in two to three days. Remember what I said earlier: Once your dog catches onto the training process, and when he has mastered just a couple of commands, new commands become easier to learn.

## "Sɪᴛ"

We covered this command along with the "come" command. However, this is another command that can be worked on at other times, such as while you're out for an evening stroll, or at any time your dog is with you and on his leash.

Have your puppy or dog near you, wearing his check collar with the indoor leash attached. Stand next to him and gently pull up on the leash while simultaneously pushing down on his rump, and in a firm voice say his name and say, "Sit." When he sits, reward with a treat and loving words. Repeat the process as many times as you can. I guarantee that after just a couple of nights or so of this, he will sit on command. You can also use this when you are teaching the "leave it" or "take" commands. Just make him sit before you give him his treat.

## "Fᴇᴛᴄʜ" ᴀɴᴅ "Dʀᴏᴘ ɪᴛ"

This is a fun exercise. Have your dog on his indoor leash—remember, we're dog whisperers, and

To teach the "sit" command, gently pull up on your dog's leash while simultaneously pushing down on his rump, and in your God-to-Moses voice say, "Sit." And don't forget the food and verbal rewards!

The "sit" training time is also a good time to teach your dog to "shake hands."

we don't set the dog up for failure—and grab a tennis ball and throw it, but no farther than he can go with the leash. Tell the dog to "Fetch" or "Get it." (Kids: If you do this indoors, make sure you have parental permission first.)

Your dog will most likely run and get the ball. If he doesn't, go with him to retrieve the ball and do it again—all the while telling him how wonderful he is. Clap your hands—make it fun! When your dog gets the ball, tell him to "come." Then tell him, "Drop it, drop it," while opening his mouth and letting the ball fall out. When the ball is on the ground, pick it up and start again. By the fourth or fifth time, I'll bet he'll be dropping the ball at your feet. This is one of the exercises that requires no food reward—the game itself is the reward.

The "drop it" command prevents the forbidden dog and human tug-of-war game. (Behavior problems connected with tug-of-war are covered in more detail in the following chapter.) The "drop it" command can also be used at other times, such as when the dog is carrying something he shouldn't have—when he's running away with one of your favorite shoes, for example. The "drop it" command is also interchangeable with the "leave it" command.

It may seem like there are a lot of rules to the Just House Manners program, but in the long run, it's as much for the dog's benefit as it is for yours. Your dog will be much happier and more secure when he knows exactly what is expected of him, and there are no confusing mixed messages coming across. As I said earlier, English is not a dog's first language, but learning simple, clear commands will enable him to learn your language, and that is very pleasing to both you and your canine. Forget the word "no" unless you attach it to a specific behavior.

While playing fetch is a good time to teach your dog to drop or release an object. This exercise does not require a food reward—the game itself is reward enough.

# CHAPTER 6

# Common Dog Behavior Problems

### *Your puppy or dog is becoming possessive of toys or snapping*

I frequently get calls from dog owners complaining that their puppy or dog is becoming possessive with his toys or is snapping at his family. Ninety percent of the time these behaviors are the direct result of playing tug-of-war, which is a common but huge mistake dog owners make.

Tug-of-war is merely a game to humans, but to canines, it's a power play. Tug-of-war is used to teach police and military canines to bite. There are specific rules to incorporate with dogs in playing tug-of-war, but most families either don't remember them or disregard them. Therefore, I recommend that you never play tug-of-war with your dog.

♣    ♣    ♣

## Your puppy is overly squirmy

Many puppies can be very squirmy to the point where you can hardly hold them. The way to make your pup calm down is to hold it close to you, tightly, firmly, snugly, all the while talking very calmly to him, saying, "Calm, calm, calm—good boy—calm, calm." The pup soon should start to calm down, and as this happens, you should then begin slowly to release your snug hold. As you relax your hold, keep giving the "calm" command, using a soft voice. If he starts to squirm again then just tighten your grip and repeat the exercise. If you have a large puppy or young adult dog you can sit on the floor for this exercise.

You can use the "calm" command whenever you want to hold the puppy and he is squirming, or when you know the puppy is anxious. This exercise should be done by adults only, not children.

♣    ♣    ♣

## Your puppy bites while playing

Most puppies do not have bite inhibition because we take them from their mothers and siblings at such an early age. If you have ever seen a litter of puppies playing and one puppy bites another, the bitten puppy yelps and runs away—play is over. Teaching your puppy bite inhibition is done in much the same way. When your puppy chomps down on you, in a loud voice yell, "Ouch!" Then put the puppy in his crate for a ten-minute time-out—play is over, and he loses the company of his human. After the time-out, let your puppy out of his crate and resume play. If he bites again repeat the loud "ouch" and plunk him back in the crate for ten minutes—game over. This method usually works after three or four times; after all, the last thing your puppy wants is to lose his time with his human. Keep in mind that the crate time itself is not the punishment—losing his human's company is the punishment.

❖  ❖  ❖

### Your dog drags you on walks

If your dog drags you down the street when you take him out for a walk, and all conventional training methods have been exhausted—and I mean *thoroughly* exhausted, including using a head halter—then this is one of the rare times that I recommend the pinch collar (also known as a prong collar).

Many people get rid of a dog that drags them down the street. The children can't walk the dog because of the pulling, or when he sees another dog, he almost pulls your arm out of its socket. If you are experiencing this problem, check with a qualified trainer before you purchase a pinch collar. This training collar gives a pinch instead of a choke and is very effective with just a flick of the wrist. You'll be amazed at how your dog responds to his already-known commands. Please consult with a professional trainer and don't get rid of your pulling dog until you have tried this training collar.

### *Your dog jumps on or sniffs guests*

Indoor-leash and on-your-rug training will go a long way toward keeping yourself and guests safe from overly enthusiastic dog greetings.

As I mentioned earlier, being pawed, sniffed, and jumped on isn't welcome from other people, and I find this behavior really rude in dogs, too. And even though a guest might laugh (albeit nervously) and tell you it's okay, believe me, it is *not* okay!

Keep in mind that to your dog, sniffing and roughhousing is not only an acceptable, but also desirable, greeting. One way to nip this canine behavior in the bud is to simply put your dog on his indoor leash and take him to the door with you when a guest arrives. Tell your dog to sit and stay, then greet your guest.

If the dog begins jumping or sniffing, however, give him a tug and again tell him to sit and stay. Explain to your guest that your dog is in training and then walk your dog to his rug and tell him, "On your rug—down, stay."

Whatever command you use will, of course, depend on how far along you are with your dog's training. If he's at the beginning of his training and you have to correct him several times for getting up from his rug and he's becoming a pest, then simply put him in his crate and give him a hard rubber treat toy with a yummy food reward on the inside.

As the visit with your guest continues, you may want to bring your dog out and try again. You'll eventually be able to just say, "On your rug—down, stay," when a guest arrives and the dog won't stir unless he's invited. More often than not, as my dog

When guests arrive, take your dog (on his indoor leash) to the door with you when you greet them. Explain that your dog is in training. After the greeting you can then send the dog to his rug, or put him in his crate if you're too busy to be with him.

sits on his rug during a visit—happy, calm, and contented—my guests can't take it any more and demand to know my secret!

Another way to stop your dog from jumping on you is to fold your hands across your chest—do not make eye contact with him—and turn your back to him. All he wants is your attention. He will run around to your front and probably try to jump again. Don't look at him and continue to turn away from him. After about fifteen to thirty seconds of keeping your back to the dog, look over your shoulder and tell him to sit. When he obeys, turn around and face him and give him a verbal reward. This method is incredible for controlling your dog's jumping on you when you let him out of his crate and he is excited to see you.

You see, if your dog jumps on you and you say "Get down" or "No," you are giving him attention. Remember, he doesn't care if the attention is negative or positive—all he wants is your attention. So, take your attention away, give him the "sit" command, and then give him your attention. It works!

### Your dog barks at and chases cars or livestock

Constant, needless barking is annoying, and chasing cars is potentially dangerous to your dog. Chasing livestock (cattle, sheep, horses, and so on) can entail even more serious consequences, especially if it involves other people's livestock, perhaps creating severe legal liabilities for the dog owner. Owners of such dogs often face a choice of taking strong action or getting rid of the pet.

As I stated at the beginning of the book, if you do your homework and research before deciding which breed of dog to get, you'll save yourself from many surprises. Many pet owners have gotten rid of their pets for annoying behavior when they really did not have to.

Although it is very controversial with animal rights activists, sometimes there is a need for drastic measures in training. I rarely recommend an electric shock collar, but it can be used to break a dog of some undesirable behavior. It is important, however, that you check with an animal behavior specialist or a very good trainer before attempting using this type of collar. Electric shock collars can be purchased at most pet supply stores and are often very effective. They emit electrical impulses mild enough that they cause neither risk nor harm to your pet, but strong enough to definitely get your dog's attention and discourage him from chasing anything you don't want him to chase. (You could use a few shots from a squirt gun, but it is less effective.) The electric shock collars really work to eliminate a dog's undesirable behavior, and they sure beat destroying your pet or surrendering it to a shelter.

Follow the directions on the collar packaging

carefully. However, if your dog is of a herding or shepherd breed and you live on a farm with livestock or horses, be prepared to deal with what is instinctive in the dog. Again, consult a professional canine trainer when considering this method.

There are alternative methods to discourage car chasing if you are truly opposed to using an electric shock collar. For example, if you have a long driveway or live on a quiet street, have a friend drive slowly away. When the dog starts to chase the car, call him by name and give one of the commands, such as "Come" or "Stay."

Repeat the process as many times as necessary, until the dog no longer chases the car. Again, this method tends to be pretty ineffective, and besides requiring more than one person, it is extremely time-consuming. In this case, it might be wise to invest in a fence.

❧ ❧ ❧

## Your dog may need behavior modification

Behavior modification usually is done for canines that are twelve months of age or older. Remember when I talked about fear periods? Behavior modification is usually required when something happened to the puppy in the first year of his life during a fear period.

Many canine trainers and veterinarians are acquiring training certification to utilize behavior modification techniques. Canine trainers must work very closely with the canine's family veterinarian when this type of service is required, and I would be cautious of a canine trainer who does not do so.

Many successful behavior modification techniques are practiced in combination with drug therapy. The drugs are commonly referred to as "doggie Prozac." However, not all behavior techniques require drug therapy. Dogs that require behavior modification techniques are dogs that display symptoms such as separation anxiety, storm fears, sudden aggression to one family member, or aggression with any human or other dogs. Many of these dogs can be helped to overcome their fears or at least become manageable.

Most behavior modification (with or without drugs) requires approximately ninety days of therapy. Why? Dogs are habitual creatures, and it requires three to four months for a behavior to become habitual. If drug therapy is required, the behavior modification process may take an additional thirty days. A dog that is anxious is a dog that cannot learn, and the drugs calm your dog so that behavior modification techniques can be learned by your dog. Several drugs are available, and your veterinarian will guide you and the canine trainer as to which one best suits your dog.

Most canines can be helped with most problems. Please don't throw in the towel until you have checked with your veterinarian and a qualified trainer to see what your options are. (Jeanette Floss, D.V.M., covers more on this subject in Chapter 10.)

### *Your dog is an aggressive biter*

I truly believe that even if you are a true, dyed-in-the-fur dog lover, no dog is worth his "gravy train" when a person—or heaven forbid, a child—is scarred emotionally or physically by a dog's bite. Some people might rationalize their dog's biting by saying, "He bites only strangers, never anyone in the family." But if that's the case in your situation, you must be prepared to confine your dog whenever you have visitors. Nowadays, people are being held liable for owning vicious, biting dogs and the legal consequences can be of real concern. If your dog shows any form of aggression, please get the advice of your veterinarian, animal behaviorist, or a qualified canine trainer right away.

I don't speak from just an abstract point of view on this topic, but from a personal standpoint. I have had to humanely terminate the lives of two of my canines for biting. Let me tell you about one of those dogs: Our family had a wonderful, Just House Manners wheaten terrier named Huey Lewis. When he was almost two years old, we had an outdoor barbecue to which we had invited about a dozen guests. Huey Lewis was having a great time visiting with everyone when, out of the blue and without provocation on anyone's part (I witnessed the entire incident), he severely bit one of our guests on the hand.

We honestly didn't know what to make of this action—could a bee have stung this dog? It was so uncharacteristic. He had never done such a thing before.

We gave the dog the benefit of the doubt and figured it was an isolated incident. Then, about two weeks later, I was feeding Huey Lewis and he viciously attacked me, biting the back of my head as I bent over to put the food in his bowl. After a trip to the emergency room—and several stitches—Huey Lewis and I made a trip to our veterinarian. Tearfully, I had the dog euthanized.

Losing this precious pet affected everyone in our family, but I could not in good conscience keep a dog that just might attack again and possibly leave worse scars than what I had suffered on someone else. Obviously, this otherwise friendly and easy-to-get-along-with canine had some internal aggression problem that surfaced as he aged, and in my opinion no amount of training could change him. This can happen to any dog, regardless of breed. Nevertheless, I believe a pet owner is ultimately responsible for overly aggressive, even dangerous, behavior. Not only should these dogs not be allowed to present potential danger to their neighborhoods, they also should not be permitted to breed and possibly pass on an aggressive gene.

Within two weeks after losing Huey Lewis, we were welcoming a new puppy into our family and were successfully on our way to achieving Just House Manners. I'm convinced that replacing Huey Lewis promptly was the right thing to do. Replacing a pet right away under such circumstances is important, especially if young children are involved. It teaches them that not all dogs bite, and that there are wonderful dogs in every breed.

# CHAPTER 7
# Fun Training and Lovable Tricks

Start fun tricks only after you and your dog have accomplished the basics. This is the time when you and your dog might want to take a clicker class.

### *"Shake hands"*

The "sit" training time is also a good time to teach your dog to "shake hands" or "give me five."

Say your dog's name and then say "shake" or "give me five" while simultaneously tapping at the back of his right front leg. When he lifts his paw grab hold of it and say "five" again, reward verbally and with a food treat. He will eventually do this automatically when he hears the command.

♣   ♣   ♣

## Clicker training

Clicker training is relatively simple to do and is a great way to train your dog. I personally love it. Many dogs (and many other types of animals) that are in the movies, as well as service dogs, are trained with this method.

To train your dog, have a bag of his favorite treats in hand along with the clicker. Press the clicker (which can be purchased at any pet supply store) to make the clicker sound to get your dog's attention, then give him a treat. Repeat this several times until the dog understands that when you click and he responds, he is rewarded with a treat. Do not use any verbal rewards during this training—you must not speak a word.

Once the dog has grasped the concept of the clicker, whenever you see a behavior that you want, such as sitting, for example, then click when the dog does that behavior and reward with a treat. Then every time the dog sits, click and reward with a treat, but still don't give verbal rewards yet. The dog will begin to sit often because he knows he is going to be rewarded with a click and a treat. Only when the dog is doing the behavior consistently may you introduce the verbal "sit" command. Eventually you won't have to use either the clicker or the food treats, just the command and a verbal reward.

Many dog behaviors can also be modified and changed with the use of a clicker, but you would need to go to a good clicker training class or study a very good clicker training book.

Many classes and many books on clicker training are available. Do a little bookstore/library research and have fun with this type of training. Many of my clients (especially those who are very busy with families, work, and so on) believe this method is too time-consuming, or they forget where they put the clicker, or some such excuse, and therefore fail at clicker training. However, if this sounds interesting to you, it's well worth a try.

### *Pulling a sled*

The temperature drops, the weatherman's prediction for three to five inches of snow was more than accurate, and the landscape becomes a winter wonderland covered with white drifts. Bolstered against the cold with mittens, boots, and snug coats, your family heads outside for wintertime fun.

Your dog, as a member of the family, can be a wonderful part of this fun, romping with you as you build snowmen and your children design snow forts.

There is more fun that you can have with your dog, though. You can teach him to pull a sled, like the dogs we see pictured in books about Holland.

Helping to get a dog into a harness and riding in a dogsled is so much fun for your children. Just be sure your dog is strong enough and the right breed to pull the weight of the sled and your child, which is really a judgment call on your part.

Your local pet supply store should carry sled harnesses—they aren't too expensive. The instructions that come with the harness will show you how to attach it to the sled. Have your dog on his outdoor leash while he is attached to the sled, and have him pull the empty sled for a few minutes just to acquaint him with the setup. Once he gets used to pulling the sled, add a little weight and get him used to pulling that weight before you let your child get in the sled. Now grab a leash and go have fun!

### Sitting up—or "Reach for the sky"

Sitting up is a fairly easy trick to teach. Although short-legged dogs have an easier time learning to sit up than those with long legs, most canines can learn to do this trick.

Sitting up should always be taught with the dog on a rug or a nonslippery floor surface, and in a corner to help keep him from tipping over while he's learning. Start by having your dog sit and then coax him to sit up by holding a choice food treat just above his nose while saying his name and "Sit up" or

"Reach for the sky." When he complies—and with a goody hovering right above his nose, he will!—give him the tidbit, along with lots of praise and love.

Once he seems confident about sitting up in the corner, bring him out into the middle of the room (still on a rug or nonslippery surface) and repeat the process until he has the hang of it. (Note: Dogs with long tails should always have them straight out behind them to help maintain their balance.)

Soon your dog will be doing this trick on his own the moment you say "Sit up" or "Reach for the sky," and hold your hand above his nose, even without food.

Isn't this fun?

🐾　　🐾　　🐾

## Saying prayers

Once your dog has learned to sit up, teaching him to "say prayers" is a snap. Sit in a straight, armless chair and have your dog sit at your side. Have him sit up and place his paws on your leg, and tell him to "stay." While holding a treat down below his paws, gently push his head down between his paws until his forehead is on or near your leg, and tell him to "say prayers."

Continue holding his head down for a while—say ten to twenty seconds—then say "amen" to signal that he can hold his head up again. Then give him his treat and lots of love.

Mac, my Border collie that I had as a teenager, loved doing this trick and would say prayers—even without being told—anytime he saw me or anyone eating something, in hopes that he would get a morsel. (Note: It's important to not overfeed your dog or overdo on snacks, so carefully read the information regarding good nutrition in the following chapter.)

Most dogs prefer to see what's going on at all times, and don't like to hide their eyes. Learning to say prayers teaches a dog obedience and submission, thus giving you more control over him. As I said earlier, the more tricks and commands your dog learns, the easier it becomes to teach him new ones. In time, most new commands and tricks can be taught in just one or two sessions.

Call the "sit up" command anything you want, such as "reach for the sky." If you do this indoors, be sure your dog is on a nonslippery surface.

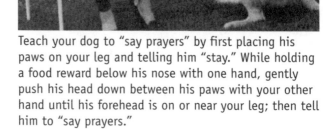

Teach your dog to "say prayers" by first placing his paws on your leg and telling him "stay." While holding a food reward below his nose with one hand, gently push his head down between his paws with your other hand until his forehead is on or near your leg; then tell him to "say prayers."

# CHAPTER 8

# Your Dog's Nutrition

I believe in good nutrition for puppies and dogs. I do not believe in dogs begging from the table. A hard-and-fast rule of mine is that when my family is eating a meal, the dogs must either be on their rugs or in their crates.

There is more to this rule than just the annoyance of being pestered while we're eating. Table scraps are not particularly good for dogs; they can easily cause dogs to become overweight and also lose out on the vitamins and balanced nutrition they really need. Veterinarian Jeanette Floss elaborates more on this in Chapter 10. Meanwhile, if you ask your vet about the wisdom of feeding from the table, I'm sure he or she will give you several other reasons why that isn't a good policy. And face it, no matter how cute or talented your pet is, your family and guests do not want a bounding dog jumping by their chair or sitting up and whining while they're trying to enjoy their steak and fries.

However, I personally think it's okay to occasionally suspend the no-table-scraps rule for outdoor dogs. Because they tend to be more active and burn up more energy, safe table scraps now and then won't interfere with their proper nutrition, nor are they as likely to become overweight. Just be sure you don't give them any kind of scraps that might be harmful to them. You might want to check with your vet on what should be avoided at all times.

Another of my rules is that I do not give my dogs little saucers of milk or let them lick our cereal bowls. My dogs are permitted to eat only from their own dishes, except when they are being rewarded with their dog cookies or other appropriate treats.

## Dog food . . . so many choices!

Once upon a time, feeding your canine was no more complicated than going to the grocery or feed store, picking up a bag of dog food, and scooping it into the dog dish once or twice a day. With a large bowl of water nearby, you were set.

Nowadays, pet foods come in so many varieties—

puppy, adult, adult active, adult inactive, and senior—you might feel like you need to have a degree in canine nutrition to know what's best for your pet. A good way to find out which dog food is best for your puppy or dog is to visit your local pet supply store and talk with the manager. With so many brands available, they usually are unbiased, and are very knowledgeable and helpful.

However, if you have an older dog or a dog with special needs, such as diabetes, consult your veterinarian regarding what kind of food is best for your pet. As mentioned earlier in the book, it is important to keep the food dishes clean, and be sure your dog has fresh water at all times. If you have outdoor dogs, be sure that they get fresh water at least twice a day in hot weather, and that their water doesn't freeze in cold weather. (And, no, it is not okay to just let your indoor dogs drink from the toilet! Think about it—yuck!)

# CHAPTER 9

# Traveling With Your Dog

You can have fun traveling with your dog, as many hotels and amusement parks these days will accommodate pets. And while there are several ways for your dog to ride in a car, the safest method is for the dog to ride in his or her crate if the crate fits into your vehicle. If that is not an option, then you'll want to teach your canine to stay on the floor of the vehicle before allowing him to ride on the seat of the car. (Needless to say, some people never allow their dogs on the seat because of dirty or wet paws and shedding fur.)

## Basic vehicle training

To teach your dog how to ride in the car, have the car's front windows down, and the passenger seat pushed all the way to the back to allow for as much floor space as possible. Walk the dog to the passenger side of the vehicle on his leash, and have him sit and stay while you open the car door. Help your dog into the car, onto the floor, and tell him again to sit and stay. Stay with the dog for a few moments to reinforce your command and to reassure him.

Next, walk around the car to the driver's side, continuing to tell your dog to sit and stay. (This is why the windows are down.)

After just a few sessions, he will learn that this is the only way to get into a car. If you decide to let him ride on the seat, you may want to protect the seat with some kind of covering, which is another use for the "on your rug—down, stay" command. Spread a large towel on the seat, say, "On your rug—down, stay," and put the dog on the towel. What the dog figures is, "Oh, my human is showing me this is my safe place," and that is where he will stay.

You may also want to protect your pet with a doggy seat belt, available at pet supply stores. If you do let your dog ride on the seat, discourage him from riding with his head out the window. More than one dog has been blinded by flying debris, or killed by another vehicle traveling too close. Not a pretty thought!

You also might want to invest in a seat belt harness. They attach to the car's existing seat belt, and come in many sizes and are relatively inexpensive. These devices are very handy in keeping your pet safe and in one place in your car.

Please keep your dog on a leash while he is in the car. Many pets have been lost or their lives have ended tragically while traveling in a car. You've invested a lot in your pet, and you want to keep him safe.

❖ ❖ ❖

### Riding in a pickup truck

And now, a word about the controversial pickup truck transportation. Many animal-rights activists believe that having a dog riding in the bed of a truck is not only dangerous, but also inhumane. Dog owners who drive pickup trucks should consider what could happen to their pet if the brakes are slammed on, if a corner is turned too sharply and quickly, or if they get rear-ended by another vehicle. Even if the dog is fastened with a leash, the animal can be strangled or have its neck broken if it is thrown from the truck.

However, if a truck is your only means of transportation, driving with your pet in the vehicle can be done relatively safely if you invest in the right equipment. Most pet supply stores carry pickup truck clamps that fit onto the truck bed's sidewalls. You

If a crate won't fit in your vehicle, the safest way for your dog to travel is on the floor of the car or in a doggie car seat. On the passenger side, help your dog into the car and onto the floor, and say, "Sit, stay." Walk around the car to the driver's side, continuing to tell your dog to sit and stay. (This is very helpful if your dog has dirty paws that you don't want on your car seats. Of course, you can invite him up anytime you want.)

will need to purchase two leashes that are about the same width as the truck bed. Attach the clamps on opposite sides and near the rear window of the truck bed. Attach the leashes to each clamp and then attach the leashes to the dog's collar. This will allow your dog to go from side to side but not over the edge. Not only will he not be thrown out if you have to make a sharp turn, but he also will not be able to jump out of the truck bed. These clamps are relatively inexpensive, and I believe they are well worth the cost if your pet is going to ride in the back of your truck. The clamps also serve as a deterrent to dog thieves, who would have to climb into the truck bed and undo the clamps, which probably would attract more attention than most thieves would like to have.

# CHAPTER 10
# When Should I See My Veterinarian?

*Jeanette Floss, D.V.M., M.S., the author of this chapter, is a specialist in theriogenology, or animal reproduction.*

In the previous chapters, Donna Chandler has given you the tools to develop and sustain a loving relationship with your dog. The purpose of this chapter is to remind you that in addition to being responsible for feeding and training, you are also responsible for his or her health and well-being.

## *Starting right*

In the past, the veterinarian was seen only as a "fixer." If a pet became sick or was injured he was taken to the doctor for care. Today's veterinarian is just as concerned about your pet's wellness. In other words, your doctor and his or her assistants can provide you with information about vaccination recommendations, annual examinations, nutrition, and screening tests to help you have a relationship with your dog well into his golden years. So shortly after (if not before) you obtain your new pet, make an appointment with your veterinarian.

In that first visit your veterinarian will discuss vaccination schedules, treatment and control of parasites, nutritional needs, routine grooming requirements, and identification options. Just as

Jeanette Floss, D.V.M., and her "girls"— Daphne, a standard poodle, and Cambre, an Airedale terrier.

with a human infant, a puppy requires a series of booster vaccinations in order to provide protection from viral diseases. Some of these diseases can be mild in nature while others can be fatal. Depending on the area of the country in which you live, whether you live in city or rural area or want to take your dog camping, hunting or just to the local park, your veterinarian will recommend the appropriate vaccinations.

❧   ❧   ❧

## Puppies and intestinal worms

Puppies can acquire intestinal parasites from their mothers. The life cycle of these worms in the mother's system allows the infective larval stages to be passed into her milk, which is then ingested by her pups. These parasites can be eliminated with medication provided by your veterinarian. Left untreated, these pups may not grow properly, may be weak or anemic, may have persistent diarrhea and may potentially spread their parasites to young children. To avoid these situations, have a fecal floatation performed at your veterinary office and treatment administered as needed. Your puppy will also be started on a monthly medication for the prevention of heartworm disease. This will be covered in more detail later in this chapter.

❧   ❧   ❧

## Puppies and nutrition

Young dogs will grow and develop rapidly in the first six months of life and therefore require higher protein and fat in their diets than adult dogs. Smaller breed dogs should be fed a quality puppy diet for at least the first eight months while larger breed puppies may require a puppy diet for up to eighteen months. Your veterinarian can give you information on diets, feeding schedules, weight maintenance, and monitoring your pet's growth.

## Grooming

Different breeds have different grooming needs. Some will need only bathing, while others will require considerable care of the skin and hair coat. Regardless of the hair type, it is important that you acquaint yourself and your pet with brushing and combing, nail trimming, ear cleaning, and oral hygiene. Dogs that swim a lot, have heavy growth of hair on their ears, or have heavy, flop-over ears may need to have their ears cleaned more frequently than dogs with erect ears. In any breed, maintenance of clean ears prevents discomfort and infection. As with young children, your puppy will lose his or her baby teeth starting around twelve to thirteen weeks of age and have a complete set of adult teeth by six months. It is a good idea to get your pet used to having his teeth examined and even brushed starting early. Your veterinarian or veterinary assistant can demonstrate the proper technique for brushing, combing, trimming nails, cleaning ears and brushing teeth. The assistant can also provide you with information about proper brushes, combs, scissors, clippers, and nail trimmers. Grooming can be an enjoyable experience for you and your pet.

## Identification and microchips

Many municipalities will assess a fine if your dog is picked up without proper identification or proof of vaccination. Your dog should have a form of permanent identification. The simplest form is an identification tag attached to the dog's collar that includes your address and phone number. Collars may become lost, which has led to the development of electronic identification devices to be injected under the skin. Most humane organizations and veterinary hospitals have electronic chip readers that can display the individual number. This number is then matched to the office implanting the chip or to the owner directly. Large numbers of missing animals are reunited with their families because of these devices. More recently a chip has been developed that can be tracked similarly to the GPS system used in automobiles. This is a great breakthrough in hunting breeds. These chips may not be available in all areas, but your veterinarian can give you information on microchip identification options available to you.

❧ ❧ ❧

## *Spaying or neutering*

Donna has already told you about the effects of spaying and neutering on behavior and training for your dog. There are also health issues to consider when electing to spay or neuter your pet. First, altering decreases the risks of developing uterine, mammary gland, and prostate disease in the older animal. Neutering also decreases the tendency for male dogs to roam, thereby avoiding potential accidents (being hit by a car, fights with other dogs or wild animals, impregnating nonspayed females, and so on). Second, the pet overpopulation problem is a nationwide issue. Every year humane organizations are overrun with unwanted or homeless dogs. Many are fortunate enough to be adopted, while many more have to be destroyed. Please do your part to prevent unwanted animal pregnancies.

More veterinarians are participating in early spay and neuter programs. Traditionally, surgery was performed when the dog reached five to six months of age. Many puppies are now being altered as early as seven to twelve weeks of age. Previously it was felt that dogs should obtain a more mature weight and size before surgery was performed to prevent undesirable changes after surgery. These included weight gain, urinary tract diseases, and reduced activity levels. It has now been shown that these conditions are not related to surgery.

On the day of surgery you can expect to bring your pet in the doctor's office in the early morning. Depending on the age of your pet, food and water should be withheld for four to twelve hours prior to surgery to prevent vomiting and aspiration during anesthesia. Dogs often go home the same day as the surgery, although your veterinarian is the best judge and may request that your pet stay overnight for observation. Your female will have an incision in the belly area that allows the doctor to remove her ovaries and entire uterus. The male dog will have a smaller incision just in front of the scrotum through which the testicles are removed. Depending on your doctor's preference, your dog may have buried or visible sutures. If visible, these stitches should be removed between ten to fourteen days after surgery.

Your veterinarian may recommend that you restrict activity to leash walking for up to ten days. This depends on your canine's personality and the preference of the doctor. Pain medication will be recommended following surgery. As with any surgery, there are inherent risks with anesthesia, bleeding, and suture failure. These risks are usually minimized with presurgical blood screening for normal organ function, customized anesthetic protocols, and cage rest.

## To breed or not to breed

If you are considering breeding your dog, you owe it to the breed and to the intended offspring to do your homework. You should have the family history back at least three generations for each parent. This includes their reproductive as well as their medical history. Be familiar with potential developmental conditions such as hip or elbow dysplasia, blindness, deafness, and bleeding disorders that are more common in some breeds.

Still other breeds have a more difficult time giving birth. These include brachycephalic breeds, or short-faced dogs with smashed-in noses. These animals have larger heads and wide shoulders with narrow hips resulting in many requiring cesarean sections. Short-faced dogs like bulldogs, Boston terriers, pugs, and Pekingese are also prone to over-heating in hot humid weather because they have small nostrils, and that can prevent the passage of air for cooling. If this condition is exaggerated, these dogs can develop severe breathing disorders as they age. In some cases, corrective surgery is necessary to open the airway. Know as much about the breed as you can before planning to produce more. Also, it is a very good idea to have prospective homes for each of the puppies you may be bringing into the world. It is your responsibility to ensure a healthy animal is placed into a loving home. If you think that allowing your dog to have a litter will help bring in more money, you are mistaken. You should never breed your dog for money.

❧   ❧   ❧

### Annual wellness examinations

After the first year of vaccinations and surgery, your veterinarian should perform a thorough health examination of your pet once a year for each year of your dog's life. Providing this service to your pet will increase the likelihood that he or she will be around for many years to come. In addition to listening to the heart and lungs, your veterinarian will examine ears, eyes, teeth, skin, weight, and internal organs. He or she may also recommend blood and urine tests to screen for underlying organ disease that may not be identified by the physical examination. An EKG and x-rays may also be recommended for the aged or geriatric pet. Many diseases or health conditions can be controlled for extended periods if identified early. Ask your veterinarian for details.

❧   ❧   ❧

### Heartworms, fleas, and ticks—oh, my!

As discussed earlier, a fecal floatation is performed to detect the presence of intestinal parasites.

A blood test should also be done to ensure that

your pet is not infected with heartworms. Heart-worms are spread through the bite of an infected mosquito. The infant worm travels from the site of the mosquito bite into the dog's bloodstream and eventually grows into a six- to eight-inch worm that lives in the upper chambers of the heart and the vessels leading to the lungs. This is a serious medical problem that can lead to heart failure and death if not treated. The good news is that this is a preventable disease, and the preventive medicine needs to be given only monthly. Many products are available through your veterinarian and can be selected based on your personal preference. Some are given orally, some are applied to the skin surface and one other variety is injected under the skin every six months.

Many products are available that will also control intestinal parasites, fleas, ticks, or mosquitoes. Pre-vention is relatively inexpensive, while treatment for heartworm disease is costly, potentially dangerous to your pet, and requires hospitalization and close monitoring for several weeks. Blood tests and x-rays will often be recommended before beginning treat-ment. Following treatment, animals are also put on severely restricted activity for four to six weeks to allow the body to eliminate all traces of the worms. Annual heartworm testing is essential for proper control and prevention of this potentially deadly disease.

External parasites such as fleas and ticks can not only make your dog uncomfortable but can also lead to disease. Flea bites are very irritating to your dog, and some will develop allergies to the bites, which in turn will result in uncontrollable scratching and cause severe damage and infection to the skin. Fleas also carry some forms of intestinal parasites. Ticks can carry viral infections that can cause weakness, anemia, and muscle and joint pain. As described above, mosquitoes can carry heartworms. Many products are available from your veterinarian for control of these external parasites. He or she can help you select the products best suited for your needs.

🐾　　🐾　　🐾

## *Vaccinations*

Vaccination boosters have traditionally been given yearly. More state agencies are now recommending a rabies vaccination every three years. Also, veterinary medical associations are also investigating whether we need annual vaccinations for other canine viral diseases. Discuss this issue with your veterinarian during your pet's annual examination to develop a vaccination schedule suitable for your pet's needs and risk potential for contracting these diseases.

♣  ♣  ♣

## Weight control

Obesity can be a sign of disease but results most often from our loving our pets to death. As Donna has mentioned, dogs are motivated by food. Owners also derive pleasure from feeding their pets. This combination of tendencies can easily lead to obesity. Regardless of the diet you are feeding, your doctor can help you with guidelines to maintain a healthy weight or reduce weight in an overweight or obese pet. In some instances a dietary change may be recommended for the maintenance of age-related conditions (heart, liver, or kidney disease), skin conditions (food sensitivity, allergies) or for performance needs.

♣  ♣  ♣

## Dental care

Dental disease is common in dogs. But proper care of the teeth can be as simple as feeding the right diet. Dogs also often accept routine brushing readily if started early in life. Preventing dental plaque and tartar will not only save your dog from gum and tooth disease and the need for painful tooth extractions, but can also protect them from other organ failures caused by bacterial infections spread from the mouth through the blood stream to the heart and kidneys. A thorough dental cleaning under anesthesia is recommended every six to twelve months. In the past, diseased teeth were simply removed; today there are specialists that can save teeth with root canals, crowns and oral surgery. Routine brushing and oral rinses will help protect your pet from tooth and gum disease, prevent pain and illness, and decrease the need for anesthetic procedures.

♣   ♣   ♣

## Behavior modification and medications—do they really help?

If you have a dog that is displaying behavior that you are concerned about, ask your veterinarian to rule out any medical reason for this behavior, such as pain, urinary infections, or organ disease. After evaluating your dog's medical condition, your veterinarian may request you have a consultation with a behavior modification specialist.

After the behaviorist has evaluated your pet, he or she will consult with your doctor to determine if medications are necessary in conjunction with training to alter the undesirable behavior. These two professionals will continue to work closely together to help you retrain your dog or correct its behavioral problems. This process may take three to four months, but remember, the medication is an aid, not a cure. The medication allows your dog to "chill out" so behavior modification techniques can take effect.

But ultimately, the success of this program rests with you, the pet owner.

Behavior modification techniques will be customized to your pet's needs. The medication selected will generally enhance your dog's ability to learn and retain the training as well as reduce some of the underlying anxiety that may have led to the behavior in the first place. There are a few side effects to the medications. You may notice your pet is tired for the first couple of days. The behaviorist will talk with you weekly on altering the behavior modification techniques slightly and then will communicate with your veterinarian approximately every fifteen to thirty days about your progress. The need for continuing the medication will be evaluated monthly. When the undesirable behavior has been corrected and your pet has responded to training, then the medication will be gradually tapered off until it is no longer needed.

## *When to seek emergency care*

Having operated an emergency hospital, I can say if you feel it is an emergency situation, then it's an emergency, and you shouldn't hesitate to take your dog to the hospital. We receive calls every day asking if a pet should be brought in. The staff and doctors cannot adequately evaluate your pet's condition without seeing it. The most common reasons pets are presented to the emergency hospital are trauma, such as being hit by cars, getting into dog fights, and falls; intoxication or poisoning; seizures; uncontrolled vomiting; or worsening signs of a pre-existing medical condition (kidney disease, heart disease, and so on). The most critical element for life is air. If your pet is having difficulty breathing, go to the hospital immediately. If your pet is bleeding, apply pressure or a bandage and notify the hospital that you are on your way. In some cases even minor disturbances may be indications of a more serious condition. You know your pet and his or her personality, behavior, and routines. If you suspect something isn't right and do not feel it can wait until a regular appointment time, you should have the pet evaluated. Never feel foolish for taking your companion and friend in for minor issues. Peace of mind for you is powerful medicine, and in some cases you may be detecting a more serious condition at its earliest stages.

### Pet health insurance

A pet comes with many responsibilities. Medical care and wellness programs can be expensive. There are several companies that provide medical insurance for your pet that will cover accidents and illness. Recently routine maintenance procedures are also covered depending on the policy purchased. Supplemental coverage may include annual vaccinations, annual dental cleanings, and spays or neuters for puppies. Conditions that may be excluded are those that can be inherited, such as hip dysplasia. Your veterinarian can provide you information on policies available in your area.

❖   ❖   ❖

## Euthanasia

Humane euthanasia or "putting your dog to sleep" is often a very difficult and heart-wrenching decision to make. In most cases it is also the most loving decision you can make for your beloved companion. The decision for euthanasia is not taken lightly by your veterinary caregivers. They are pet owners too. You have shared a life and relationship with your pet and in the end you want their passing to be painless and dignified. How you deal with the passing of a cherished family member is very personal as well. Your veterinarian will do all in his or her power to provide a quiet environment for you and your family to visit; often, if you wish, you can be present for the procedure.

An injection is given that deeply sedates your pet; then your pet's breathing and heart slow and stop. The process is very quick, painless, and free of anxiety for your pet. There are many options available to you and your family for memorials, burials, and cremations. A pet can never be replaced, but the love and devotion they give is everlasting.

# Epilogue

Now you and your dog are on your own!

I hope that this book will provide you with a lifelong plan for your new canine member of the family.

Some key points to remember: Once you start trusting your dog outside his crate, and without his indoor leash, if he makes a mistake, all you'll probably need to do is give him a refresher course in his crate and indoor-leash training. Wait about a week before turning him loose again. And remember also that the training can't really sink in with very young pups, so don't give your dog his freedom before he's old enough to be able to handle it.

Once your canine has begun his command training, take him with you everywhere as much as possible. He will love being with you—and your family—and it will also socialize him and enhance all his training methods. Remember, he has your last name!

By properly and faithfully using the Just House Manners plan, I'm confident that your canine will never be one of those tragic creatures that ends up in the local humane society or dog pound, or worse, just dumped at the roadside.

Sharing a home with an animal and loving and caring for it adds value and depth to a person's life, and what it can add to a child's life is immeasurable. Pets can so greatly improve quality of life and mental attitudes that it is becoming a standard practice to take animals to visit nursing homes, hospice programs, and children's hospitals, and arranging for dogs and cats for shut-ins to care for. My friend Carol Barker and Cletus, her certified therapy dog, share their love once a week in a local extended care facility in Dayton, Ohio. Carol finds that this is a way she can give back to our society utilizing her cherished pet—a reward for both.

The unconditional love that pets offer often brings people out of themselves, generally leaving them happier and feeling that life is more worthwhile. Animals also seem to have a sixth sense about people, knowing not only whom to trust, but also what person seems to need attention and love the most. If you have children between the ages of nine and eighteen, I encourage you to check out your local 4-H. Most 4-H programs include dog obedience, agility, and confirmation training. These programs have been proven many times over to be successful for both child and dog. My son Austin is very involved with 4-H and he loves every minute of it.

I am convinced that if you've never experienced the special bond of love that you can share with an animal, then you're missing something truly wonderful. If that's the case, and you are reading this book, then you're probably ready to start on this marvelous adventure.

So, get ready for a wonderful treat. Remember to share these training methods with your children, beginning with "dog English." But don't loan this book to your friends—you'll need it when you decide you want a second dog!

Carol Barker and her canine family, Cletus (in front) and Callie.

In closing, I'd like to leave you with another nugget of my own personal philosophy: Any time you plan to do business with someone, ask whether he or she is an animal lover. My experience has taught me that if someone is a true animal lover, that person tends not to be overly selfish or self-centered and is worthy and capable of receiving and giving trust and love.

Now, relax while you discover the rewards of owning a good dog—one with Just House Manners!

# Index

# BOOKS OF INTEREST

## Everybody Loves Ice Cream
by Shannon Jackson Arnold

Three scoops please: a travel book, a cookbook and a pop culture history all in one, the most complete treatment of the subject a reader can find anywhere. Whether you're looking for a great ice-cream stand nearby, a recipe for rocky road, or an explanation for what makes an ice cream "super-premium," you'll find it here. It's true that *Everybody Loves Ice Cream,* and this book tells you why.

Packed with photos and designed with mix-ins and toppings of all sorts, this charming book is like a trip to the soda fountain—something everybody enjoys. Author Shannon Jackson Arnold covers everything from a factory tour to homemade recipes, from definitions for various frozen desserts to soda jerk jargon.

*Everybody Loves Ice Cream* provides readers with a parfait look at every aspect of our favorite frozen treat:

- what's the best and where to get it, across the country
- how to make delicious ice cream yourself
- how the manufacturers make it
- where and how it was invented and how it has evolved
- how it has played a part in American culture

Step right up for a taste of the sweetest book ever!

**Shannon Jackson Arnold** is a freelance writer and editor living in Milwaukee, Wisconsin. Her work appears in many magazines, including *Marie Clare* and *Wisconsin Trails,* and she is the former editor of *Ohio* magazine.

Paperback, 4-color throughout, 8 ¾ x 8 ¾
Price: $19.99    ISBN: 1-57860-165-7

To order call: 1(800) 343-4499 www.emmisbooks.com
**EMMIS BOOKS 1700 MADISON ROAD CINCINNATI, OHIO 45206**

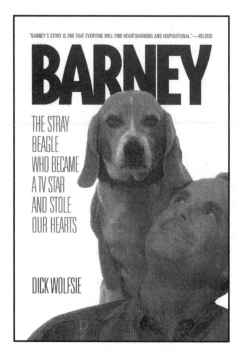

## Barney: The Stray Beagle Who Became a TV Star and Stole Our Hearts

By Dick Wolfsie

Running out the door one very cold morning, TV reporter Dick Wolfsie nearly tripped over the tiny beagle shivering on his front doorstep. His heart went out to the little stray, and he welcomed the dog into the house before going off to work. While Dick was gone, Barney destroyed the couch, a pair of high heels, the curtains and the living room rug. Dick's wife issued an ultimatum: "The dog must go. Either that, or you have to take him to work with you."

So began a street mutt's transformation into a TV celebrity and Indiana's favorite dog. Borne out of a family's destruction, Barney's career in the public eye included 3,000 shows and 12 straight years on the air, four times longer that most network sitcoms. Barney starred in 14 commercials, had drinks and sandwiches named after him at local restaurants and had a special suite at the local kennel. He visited hospitals, retirement homes and schools. Barney also had his own late-night movie show and a line of boxer shorts with his picture. Many believe he was the most recognizable personality at Channel 8, where Dick filled in as his side-kick. And no one ever mistook him for someone else.

When Barney died, Dick received 1,700 e-mails and letters expressing sympathy and condolences. A popular author of a number of books, Dick Wolfsie recounts here the greatest Barney moments. Packed with photos, letters from fans, and Dick's touching commentary, *BARNEY* is destined to make all of his fans laugh, cry and howl at the moon.

Paperback    Price: $14.99
ISBN: 1-57860-167-3

To order call: 1(800) 343-4499 www.emmisbooks.com

**EMMIS BOOKS  1700 MADISON ROAD  CINCINNATI, OHIO 45206**